David Gasperetti

University of Notre Dame

A Reference Grammar for

В пути

Russian Grammar in Context

Second Edition

Olga Kagan
University of California, Los Angeles

Frank Miller
Columbia University, New York

Ganna Kudyma
University of South California, Los Angeles

PEARSON
Prentice
Hall

woRLd
Languages

Upper Saddle River, New Jersey 07458

Copyright © 2006 by Pearson Education, Inc.
Upper Saddle River, New Jersey 07458

Printed in the United States of America
10 9 8 7

ISBN 0-13-189921-X

Table of Contents

Foreword

How to Use this Reference Grammar

The main purpose of the *Reference Grammar* is to provide students with an overview of Russian grammar by putting all the information for each grammatical category covered in *В пути* in one place.

The *Reference Grammar* was created with three principles in mind. First, it is not meant to replace the grammar explanations given in *В пути* but rather to complement them. This principle leads directly to the second one: the *Reference Grammar* contains **all** the grammar presented in the textbook. In other words, students who consult this grammar on any topic can be confident they will find the same information and general approach to grammar as in *В пути*. (Page references to corresponding explanations in the textbook are given in parentheses.) If there is any deviation from the way grammar is presented in the textbook, it is in order to give **additional** information. Third, given that students will consult the textbook for grammar explanations before looking into the *Reference Grammar*, more responsibility is placed on the student to make connections between various grammatical concepts. One of the most notable examples of this approach concerns the charts that list noun and adjective endings for each case, where only the ending that would be used for hard stems is given. For instance, only -**ы** is given as the nominative plural ending for masculine and feminine nouns rather than -**ы**/-**и**, and only -**ой** is given as the feminine singular adjective ending in genitive, prepositional, dative, and instrumental case rather than -**ой**/-**ей**. Not only does this approach simplify the process of memorizing case endings, it also encourages students to internalize the relationship between case endings, spelling rules, the hardness and softness of Russian consonants, and the dual symbols—such as **ы**/**и**—for each Russian vowel.

The *Reference Grammar* will be most useful to students the more they need to take a long view of Russian grammar and see each topic as a total system. This will most likely be the case when they study for chapter tests and final exams or when they want to review material they have covered in previous chapters. At the end of the semester the *Reference Grammar* is an ideal tool to use for a comprehensive review. Since it covers all the grammar introduced in the textbook, students can be certain that they have collected before them everything they need to know for this aspect of the course. For example, instead of going through Chapters 1, 2, 3, and 4 in the textbook to retrieve all the information on the large category of genitive case, students may refer to the seven-page chapter in the *Reference Grammar* that treats this subject in its entirety. The same advantage holds when students are studying for tests on individual chapters. For instance, Chapter 5 in *В пути* contains information on the use of aspect in the future tense. If students wish to see how this information fits in with the total presentation of aspect throughout the textbook, they may do so by reviewing the brief chapter "Verbs: Aspect" in the *Reference Grammar*. Moreover, throughout the semester students may use the *Reference Grammar* to refresh their command of any grammatical topic introduced in *В пути*. For instance, if, during the second semester of the course, students find they are still struggling with certain aspects of expressing clock time, they can refer to the appropriate chapter in the grammar and find there all the information that is introduced over the course of two chapters in the textbook. In this regard, the *Reference Grammar* provides a handy way for students to review and reinforce their knowledge of any and all material they have already covered during the semester or even the entire academic year. If, as the Russians say, "Повторе́ние—мать уче́ния," then allotting fifteen to thirty minutes per week to a review of the topics contained in the *Reference Grammar* will be time well spent.

Acknowledgments

First and foremost, I would like to thank Olga Kagan and Frank Miller for the time, energy, and creativity they put into the first edition of *B nymu*. Over the four years I have been using *B nymu* in my intermediate Russian classes, I have found that it virtually teaches itself. Without the great investment of talent on the part of the authors—and their new collaborator for the second edition, Ganna Kudyma—the *Reference Grammar* would not have been possible. I am especially indebted to Olga Kagan for her many suggestions regarding style and usage and to Frank Miller for helping me solve any number of problems, including the challenge of putting accent marks into Cyrillic texts. Their insights and patience were appreciated in equal measure.

I am also indebted to the authors and to Pearson Prentice Hall publishers for their support of this project. Rachel McCoy, Acquisitions Editor for World Languages, and Meriel Martinez Moctezuma, Supplements Editor, have always been supportive and quick to respond to queries and problems. At Notre Dame, I am most grateful for the talents of my two undergraduate research assistants—Shelece Easterday, whose keen eye spotted many typos and problems in formatting, and Sheila Dawes, whose independent judgment, patience, and attention to detail were invaluable in preparing the final drafts of the manuscript. Among my colleagues, I would also like to thank Katie English for her technical assistance with the computer problems that arose as a result of this project and Svitlana Kobets for her help with questions of style. I wish to express my gratitude as well to Irina Iourtaeva, whose expertise in the language served as the penultimate check of the manuscript, and Karen Hohner, whose meticulous reading of the final draft improved this project significantly. I am indebted to all of the above for the help and insights they have provided me while fully acknowledging that any remaining mistakes and oversights are my responsibility.

I dedicate this work to George Smalley and Melvin Strom, my first teachers of Russian, who fostered in me an appreciation for the structure of language.

The Vowel Chart and Hard vs. Soft Consonants

Spelling Rules

I. The Vowel Chart and Hard vs. Soft Consonants

Russian has five vowels but uses ten vowel symbols to express the hardness or softness of a preceding consonant. The vowel symbols can be grouped into pairs, as in this chart:

э	ы	а	о	у
е	и	я	ё	ю

A. If one of the vowels above the line follows a consonant, the consonant will be pronounced "hard"; if one of the vowels below the line follows a consonant, the consonant will be pronounced "soft." For example, the д in да́же is hard, and both д's in дя́дя are soft.

B. If no vowel follows a consonant, it is pronounced "hard" unless it is followed by a soft sign (ь), in which case it is pronounced "soft." For example, the т in кот is hard, but the т in гость is soft.

Note: It is important to remember that three consonants in Russian—ж, ш, ц—are always hard, and three consonants—й, ч, щ—are always soft, no matter which vowel symbol comes after them. Other consonants can be hard or soft, depending on what comes after them (vowel, soft sign, consonant, nothing).

II. Spelling Rules

A. Spelling Rule Number One: ы (yeri) should not be written after the consonants к, г, х (the velars) and ж, ч, ш, щ (the hushers): instead write и. Thus, even though the noun парк ends in a hard consonant and would normally take ы as an ending in the nominative plural, because of spelling rule number one, the nominative plural is па́рки.

B. Spelling Rule Number Two: Unstressed о should not be written after any **soft** consonant, the "**hushing**" consonants (ж, ч, ш, and щ), and the consonant ц. In these situations replace it with **е**. That is why we can render a soft-stem neuter noun like мо́ре this way (in the following example an apostrophe represents the softness of the preceding consonant)—мо́р'-о—to show that it has a soft **р** but still has the neuter ending **о**. In writing, after the soft **р** the unstressed **о** will be written as **е** (мо́ре).

Note: At times, the spelling rules conflict with the rules for using the vowel chart to determine the hard vs. soft pronunciation of consonants. For example, the Russian word "to live" is spelled **жить**. Given spelling rule number one, we must write **и** after **ж**, and therefore it would seem that **ж** should be pronounced soft, since it is followed by an **и**. However, since **ж** is one of three Russian consonants that is always hard, the word must be **pronounced** as though the **ж** were followed by the vowel symbol **ы**.

C. Spelling and the Consonant й

Spelling Rule Number Three: Whenever **й** is followed by a vowel (with the exception of a few words of foreign derivation), it will **not** appear in writing. Instead, the combination of **й + vowel** will be replaced by the corresponding vowel symbol **below the line** in the vowel chart:

э	ы	а	о	у
е	и	я	ё	ю

For example, **й + а = я**: музе́**й** + **а** = музе́**я**; **й + о = е** (unstressed after the soft consonant **й**; **see** spelling rule two, above): музе́**й** + **ом** = музе́**ем**.

Имени́тельный паде́ж—Nominative Case

I. Оконча́ния—Endings

A. Существи́тельные—Nouns (pp. 7–8, 62)

Endings

Падежи́ Cases	Мужско́й и сре́дний род		Же́нский и мужско́й род	Же́нский и сре́дний род		Множ. число́ м./ж. ср.	
Имени́тельный **Nominative**	**-#**	**-о**	**-а**	**-#**	**-а**	**-ы**	**-а**
Вини́тельный Accusative	Inanimate = Nom. Animate = Gen.		-у	Like Nominative		Inanimate = Nom. Animate = Gen.	
Роди́тельный Genitive	-а		-ы	-и		-#/-ей/-ов	
Предло́жный Prepositional	-е/-и[1]		-е/-и[1]	-и		-ах	
Да́тельный Dative	-у		-е/-и[1]	-и		-ам	
Твори́тельный Instrumental	-ом		-ой	-ью	-ом	-ами	

Examples

Мужско́й и сре́дний род		Жен. и муж. род	Же́нский и сре́дний род		Мно́жественное число́ муж./жен. сре́дний	
-#	**-о**	**-а**	**-#**	**-а**	**-ы**	**-а**
стол					столы́	
день					дни	
нож					ножи́	
ге́ний					ге́нии	
оте́ц					отцы́	
	окно́					о́кна
	мо́ре					моря́
	зда́ние					зда́ния
		сестра́			сёстры	
		пе́сня			пе́сни	
		кни́га			кни́ги	
		пе́нсия			пе́нсии	
		дя́дя (м.)			дя́ди	
			дверь		две́ри	
				и́мя		имена́

[1] Nouns ending in -ий, -ие, or -ия take the ending -и in these cases; other nouns take the ending -е.

Nouns: How to Handle Stems and Endings

Virtually all Russian nouns consist of a **stem** that ends in a consonant and an **ending** that is, or begins with, a vowel. The stem carries the basic meaning of the word ("table," "book," "place"), and the ending expresses gender, case, and number. In the nominative singular, most masculine nouns are stem only, with a zero (#)—or, in other words, no—ending. (In the following chart an apostrophe ['] represents the softness of the preceding consonant.)

Masculine/Мужско́й род			Neuter/Сре́дний род			Feminine/Же́нский род		
Stem	Ending	Word	Stem	Ending	Word	Stem	Ending	Word
стол	-#	= стол	мéст	-о	= мéсто	книг	-а	= книга
учи́тел'	-#	= учи́тель	мóр'	-о	= мóре	пéсн'	-а	= пéсня
гéний	-#	= гéний	зда́ний	-о	= зда́ние	лéкций	-а	= лéкция

Note: It is easy to see that a masculine noun like гéний has a stem ending in -ий, since in the nominative case masculine nouns have no ending (they end in a bare stem). Because of spelling rule 3 below, however, we cannot tell from the nominative case of the word that neuter nouns like зда́ние and feminine nouns like лéкция also have stems ending in -ий. If we keep spelling rule 3 in mind when dealing with nouns ending in -ие and -ия, however, the true stem type (and declension pattern) of these types of nouns will be clear.

Note: Keep these **SPELLING RULES** in mind with respect to any Russian word.

> 1. **ы** (yeri) should not be written after the consonants **к, г, х** (the velars) and **ж, ч, ш, щ** (the hushers): instead write **и**. Thus, even though the noun парк ends in a hard consonant and would normally take **ы** as an ending in the nominative plural, because of this spelling rule, the nominative plural is па́рки.

> 2. Unstressed **о** should not be written after any **soft** consonant, the "**hushing**" consonants (**ж, ч, ш,** and **щ**), and the consonant **ц**. In these situations, replace it with **е**. That is why a soft-stem neuter noun like мо́ре can be rendered as мо́р'-о to show that it has a soft **р** (an apostrophe represents the softness of a consonant) but still has the neuter ending **о**. In writing, after the soft **р** the unstressed **о** will be written as **е** (мо́ре).

> 3. The Consonant **й**: Whenever **й** is followed by a vowel (with the exception of a few words of foreign derivation), it will **not** appear in writing. Instead, the combination of **й** + **vowel** will be replaced by the corresponding vowel symbol **below the line** in this chart:

$$\frac{\text{э} \quad \text{ы} \quad \text{а} \quad \text{о} \quad \text{у}}{\text{е} \quad \text{и} \quad \text{я} \quad \text{ё} \quad \text{ю}}$$

> For example, **й** + **а** = **я**: лéкций + а = лéкция; **й** + **о** = **е** (unstressed after the soft consonant **й**; **see** spelling rule 2 above): зда́ний + о = зда́ние.

Nouns: Types of Nouns that Don't Decline

1. **Russian words of foreign origin ending in certain vowels,** such as -е, -и, -о, and -ю: Examples include кафé, такси́, метрó, and меню́. Most of these words are neuter.

2. **Place names for foreign** cities, states, and countries: If such words end in a consonant, they are masculine and decline like стол or день; if they end in -a or -я, they are feminine and decline like сестра́, пéсня, or пéнсия. (Some nouns, like Гава́йи [Hawaii], decline like a plural noun.)

Otherwise, nouns in this category are indeclinable. For example, Вашингто́н, Индиа́на, and Вирги́ния decline, but Ога́йо and Теннесси́ do not. (p. 29)

3. **Non-Russian first names:** Masculine names decline if they end in a consonant, and feminine names decline if they end in -a or -я. For example, Бил, Ба́рбара, and Патри́ция decline, but Джо and Мэ́ри do not.

Nominative Plural Endings for Nouns (p. 62)

Masculine and feminine nouns use **-ы** to denote the nominative plural after hard consonants and **-и** after soft consonants, the velars (**к, г, х**), and the "hushers" (**ж, ч, ш, щ**) (**see** spelling rule 1, above). Neuter nouns take an **-а** ending in the nominative plural after hard consonants and **-я** after soft consonants. (In the following chart an apostrophe ['] represents the softness of the preceding consonant.)

	Masculine/Муж. род		Neuter/Сред. род		Feminine/Жен. род	
Stem Type	Singular	Plural	Singular	Plural	Singular	Plural
Hard	стол-#	столы́	ме́ст-о	места́	сестр-а́	сёстры
Velars	парк-#	па́рки			кни́г-а	кни́ги
Soft	ден'-#	дни	мо́р'-о	моря́	пе́сн'-а	пе́сни
	музе́й-#	музе́и			двер'-#	две́ри
Hushers	гара́ж-#	гаражи́			да́ч-а	да́чи
-ий stems	ге́ний-#	ге́нии	зда́ний-о	зда́ния	пе́нсий-а	пе́нсии

Note the changes in the nominative plurals of the following nouns.

Masculine Nouns/Мужско́й род

Stressed -а́			-ья			Different Form		
Singular		Plural	Singular		Plural	Singular		Plural
ве́чер	→	вечера́	брат	→	бра́тья	ребёнок	→	де́ти
дом	→	дома́	стул	→	сту́лья	челове́к	→	лю́ди
го́род	→	города́	муж	→	мужья́			
па́спорт	→	паспорта́	друг	→	друзья́			
учи́тель	→	учителя́	сын	→	сыновья́			
профе́ссор	→	профессора́						

Masculine/Мужско́й род -ёнок → -я́та;[2] -анин → -ане[2]			Neuter/Сре́дний род -ен- Suffix[3]			Feminine/Же́нский род -ер- Suffix[4]		
Singular		Plural	Singular		Plural	Singular		Plural
котёнок (#)	→	котя́та	и́мя	→	имена́	мать	→	ма́тери
англича́нин (#)	→	англича́не	вре́мя	→	времена́	дочь	→	до́чери

---

[2] These words represent two groups of nouns. Nouns ending in -онок/-ёнок generally represent young animals, for example: цыплёнок (baby chick) and медвежо́нок (bear cub). Ребёнок (baby, child) falls into this category, but it has the standard plural form of де́ти. The plural form ребя́та exists, but it has the meaning of "guys," "kids," "boys and girls." Nouns ending in -анин/-янин designate a person from a certain place, such as киевля́нин (an inhabitant of Kiev) or армяни́н (Armenian). **See** the chapter "Nouns: Sample Declensions," section I, for the entire declension pattern, both singular and plural, of these two types of nouns.

[3] There are eight other nouns in this category of third-declension neuter nouns, including пла́мя (flame) and пле́мя (tribe).

[4] мать and дочь are the only two nouns in this category.

B. Прилага́тельные—Adjectives (pp. 62, 349)

Endings

Падежи́ Cases	Мужско́й и сре́дний род		Же́нский род	Мно́жественное число́
Имени́тельный **Nominative**	**-ЫЙ** **-О́Й**[5]	**-ое**	**-ая**	**-ые**
Вини́тельный Accusative	Inanimate = Nom. Animate = Gen.		-УЮ	Inanimate = Nom. Animate = Gen.
Роди́тельный Genitive	-ОГО		-ОЙ	-ЫХ
Предло́жный Prepositional	-ОМ		-ОЙ	-ЫХ
Да́тельный Dative	-ОМУ		-ОЙ	-ЫМ
Твори́тельный Instrumental	-ЫМ		-ОЙ	-ЫМИ

Examples

	Мужско́й и сре́дний род		Же́нский род	Мно́жественное число́
Stem	**-ЫЙ** **-О́Й**[5]	**-ое**	**-ая**	**-ые**
Hard Stems	но́вый	но́вое	но́вая	но́вые
Soft Stems	си́ний	си́нее	си́няя	си́ние
к, г, х Stems	плохо́й	плохо́е	плоха́я	плохи́е
ж, ч, ш, щ Stems	хоро́ший	хоро́шее	хоро́шая	хоро́шие

C. Местоиме́ния-прилага́тельные—Special Modifiers (pp. 348–49)

мой (твой, свой)	мой	моё	моя́	мои́
наш (ваш)	наш	на́ше	на́ша	на́ши
весь	весь	всё	вся	все
э́тот	э́тот	э́то	э́та	э́ти
тот	тот	то	та	те
чей	чей	чьё	чья	чьи
оди́н	оди́н	одно́	одна́	одни́

---

[5] When the ending is stressed, the masculine nominative singular adjective ending is -о́й, otherwise it is -ый.

II. Употребле́ния имени́тельного падежа́—The Uses of Nominative Case

Nominative case . . .

A. answers the questions **Кто?** and **Что?** and denotes the **subject** of a sentence or clause (p. 61).

1. **Кто** рабо́тает в магази́не? В магази́не рабо́тает моя́ дочь (#).
Who works in the store? **My daughter** works in the store.

2. **Что** лежи́т на столе́? На столе́ лежи́т ру́сский журна́л (#).
What is on the table? **A Russian magazine** is on the table.

Note: Since word order in Russian is not fixed, the subject does not always come at the beginning of the sentence. Generally, what is already known (that is, "old" information) comes first in a Russian sentence, and unknown (or "new") information comes after it. In sentences 1 and 2 above, the subject is at the end of the sentence because in both instances it represents new information. In sentence 1, for example, we know from the question that someone is working in a store. In the answer, this is old information and therefore comes first (В магази́не рабо́тает . . .). The new information, which directly answers the question "Who?" (Кто?), comes at the end of the sentence (. . . моя́ дочь). (p. 63)

B. denotes the **predicate** of a sentence (a noun, pronoun, adjective, or number)[6] after the unexpressed present tense of the verb "to be" (быть). Both the subject and predicate of the sentence are in nominative case. (p. 61)

1. Мои́ сыновья́ — врачи́. My sons are **doctors**.[7]
2. На́ша маши́на — ста́рая. Our car is **old**.

C. is used for nouns and pronouns after the introductory word э́то ("This is. . ."; "These are . . ."). (p. 61)

1. Э́то Ива́н (#) Ива́нович (#). This is **Ivan Ivanovich**.
2. Э́то мои́ до́чери. These are **my daughters**.

D. is used to indicate which **day** of the month it is. The month is given in genitive case. (p. 44)

1. Како́е сего́дня число́? Сего́дня пятна́дцатое октября́.[8]
What is today's **date**? Today is **the fifteenth** of October.

2. Како́е вчера́ бы́ло число́? Вчера́ бы́ло второ́е ию́ня.
What was yesterday's **date**? Yesterday was **the second** of June.

3. Како́е за́втра бу́дет число́? За́втра бу́дет седьмо́е февраля́.
What is tomorrow's **date**? Tomorrow will be **the seventh** of February.

---

[6] **See** the chapter "Sentence Structure," section I, B, in this grammar for information on predicates.
[7] **Remember:** to express what someone does (for a living or occupation), use the pronoun кто. Кто он/она́? (What does he/she do?)
[8] Just as in English, in Russian the word for "date" (число́) is used in the question but not in the answer.

Вини́тельный паде́ж—Accusative Case

I. Оконча́ния—Endings

A. Существи́тельные—Nouns (pp. 17, 68–69, 99)

Endings

Падежи́ Cases	Мужско́й и сре́дний род		Же́нский и мужско́й род	Же́нский и сре́дний род		Множ. число́ м./ж. ср.	
Имени́тельный Nominative	-#	-о	-а	-#	-а	-ы	-а
Вини́тельный Accusative	Inanim. = Nom. Animate = Gen.		**-у**	Like Nominative		Inanim. = Nom. Animate = Gen.	
Роди́тельный Genitive	-а		-ы	-и		-#/-ей/-ов	
Предло́жный Prepositional	-е/-и[1]		-е/-и[1]	-и		-ах	
Да́тельный Dative	-у		-е/-и[1]	-и		-ам	
Твори́тельный Instrumental	-ом		-ой	-ью	-ом	-ами	

Examples

Мужско́й и сре́дний род			Жен. и муж. род	Же́нский и сре́дний род		Мно́жественное число́ муж./жен. сре́дний	
-#/-а	**-о**	**-у**		**-#**	**-а**	**-ы -#/-ов/-ей**	**-а**
стол						столы́	
день						дни	
учи́теля						учителе́й	
нож						ножи́	
отца́						отцо́в	
	окно́						о́кна
	мо́ре						моря́
	зда́ние						зда́ния
		сестру́				сестёр	
		пе́сню				пе́сни	
		кни́гу				кни́ги	
		пе́нсию				пе́нсии	
		дя́дю (м.)				дя́дей	
			дверь			две́ри	
					и́мя		имена́

[1] Nouns ending in -ий, -ие, or -ия take the ending -и in these cases; other nouns take the ending -е.

B. Прилага́тельные—Adjectives (pp. 69, 99)

Endings

Падежи́ Cases	Мужско́й и сре́дний род		Же́нский род	Мно́жественное число́
Имени́тельный Nominative	-ый/-о́й[2]	-ое	-ая	-ые
Вини́тельный **Accusative**	**Inanimate = Nom.** **Animate = Gen.**		**-ую**	**Inanimate = Nom.** **Animate = Gen.**
Роди́тельный Genitive	-ого		-ой	-ых
Предло́жный Prepositional	-ом		-ой	-ых
Да́тельный Dative	-ому		-ой	-ым
Твори́тельный Instrumental	-ым		-ой	-ыми

Examples

	Мужско́й и сре́дний род		Же́нский род	Мно́жественное число́
Stem	**-ый;-о́й[2]/** **-ого**	**-ое**	**-ую**	**-ые/-ых**
Hard Stems	но́вый/ но́вого	но́вое	но́вую	но́вые/но́вых
Soft Stems	си́ний/ си́него	си́нее	си́нюю	си́ние/си́них
к, г, х Stems	плохо́й/ плохо́го	плохо́е	плоху́ю	плохи́е/плохи́х
ж, ч, ш, щ Stems	хоро́ший/ хоро́шего	хоро́шее	хоро́шую	хоро́шие/хоро́ших

C. Местоиме́ния-прилага́тельные—Special Modifiers (pp. 69, 99)

мой (твой, свой)	мой/моего́	моё	мою́	мои́/мои́х
наш (ваш)	наш/на́шего	на́ше	на́шу	на́ши/на́ших
весь	весь/всего́	всё	всю	все/всех
э́тот	э́тот/э́того	э́то	э́ту	э́ти/э́тих
тот	тот/того́	то	ту	те/тех
чей	чей/чьего́	чьё	чью	чьи/чьих
оди́н	оди́н/одного́	одно́	одну́	одни́/одни́х

---

[2] When the ending is stressed, the masculine nominative singular adjective ending is -о́й, otherwise it is -ый.

II. Употребле́ния вини́тельного падежа́—The Uses of Accusative Case

Accusative case . . .

A. answers the question **Куда́?** with the prepositions **в** and **на**.[3]

Note: Nouns using **в** in prepositional case use **в** in accusative case, and nouns using **на** in prepositional case use **на** in accusative case.

Они́ **на** рабо́те. = They are **at** work.	Они́ иду́т **на** рабо́ту. = They are going **to** work.
Они́ **в** шко́ле. = They are **at** school.	Они́ иду́т **в** шко́лу. = They are going **to** school.

1. After a verb expressing motion, **в** = "in(to)" or "to" (generally used with nouns denoting closed or covered spaces), and **на** = "on" (p. 16).

    a. Я положи́л кни́гу **в** стол (#). I put the book **in(to) the desk**.
    b. Они́ иду́т **в** библиоте́ку. They are going **to (into) the library**.
    c. Он сел **на** стул (#). He sat down **on the chair**.

2. However, **на** can also mean "in(to)" or "to" with nouns that fall into the categories noted below (p. 10). For example, Они идут/едут . . .

Open Spaces

на пло́щадь (#)	to the square
на стадио́н (#)	to the stadium
на у́лицу	to the street
на остано́вку	to the bus stop
на ста́нцию	to the metro station

Functions and Events

на (футбо́льный) ма́тч (#)	to the (soccer) game
на у́жин (за́втрак, обе́д [#])	to supper (breakfast, dinner)
на конце́рт (#), **на** о́перу	to the concert, to the opera
на фи́льм (#), **на** ле́кцию	to the film, to the lecture
на дискоте́ку	to the disco

School Terms

на ка́федру	to the department
на курс (#)	to the course
на факульте́т (#)	to the department
на уро́к (#)	to the lesson
на заня́тие	to the class
на заня́тия (pl.)	to classes; to school
на экза́мен (#)	to the exam
на контро́льную рабо́ту	to the test

Compass Points

на восто́к (#)	to the east
на за́пад (#)	to the west
на се́вер (#)	to the north
на юг (#)	to the south

Seas, Oceans, Rivers, Lakes, Islands

на Чёрное мо́ре	to the Black Sea
на Ти́хий океа́н (#)	to the Pacific Ocean
на Во́лгу	to the Volga
на Байка́л (#)	to Lake Baikal
на Ку́бу, **на** Гава́йи (pl.)	to Cuba, to Hawaii

Certain States and Countries

на Аля́ску	to Alaska
на Гава́йи (pl.)	to Hawaii
на Ку́бу	to Cuba
на/в Украи́ну	to Ukraine

And These Commonly-Used Words

на вокза́л (#)	to the train station
на да́чу	to the dacha
на заво́д (#)	to the plant/factory
на Кавка́з (#)	to the Caucasus
на по́чту	to the post office

на рабо́ту	to work
на Ура́л (#)	to the Ural Mountains
на фа́брику	to the factory
на (тре́тий) эта́ж (#)	to (the third) floor

---

[3] For a review of prepositions governing accusative case, **see** section II, D, below.

3. **But**, use **в** with nouns denoting cities, states, and countries (except those noted in section II, A, 2, above) and the word for university (p. 9).

    a. Они́ летя́т **в** Москву́. They are flying **to Moscow**.

    b. Она́ е́дет **в** Виско́нсин (**#**). She is driving **to Wisconsin**.

    c. Мы пла́вали **в** Росси́ю. We sailed **to Russia**.

    d. Я е́ду **в** Аме́рику. I am going **to America**.

    e. Ру́сские фи́зики иду́т **в** университе́т (**#**).
The Russian physicists are walking **to the university**.

Note the correspondences between prepositions. The prepositions for going "to/in(to)/on," being "at/in/on," and coming "from" are linked in the following way (pp. 23, 35):

	motion to **Куда́?**	*position in/at/on* **Где?**	*motion from* **Отку́да?**
For Places	**В** + ACC. **НА** + ACC.	**В** + PREP. **НА** + PREP.	**ИЗ** + GEN. **С** + GEN.
For People	**К** + DAT.	**У** + GEN.	**ОТ** + GEN.

B. expresses **the direct object**. The direct object is the person or thing (noun or pronoun) at which the action of the verb is directed. (p. 70)

    1. Я ви́жу учи́тельницу. I see **the teacher**.
(The action of the verb "see" is directed at the noun "teacher.")

    2. Она́ чита́ет ру́сский журна́л (**#**). She is reading **a Russian magazine**.
(The action of the verb "read" is directed at the noun "magazine.")

C. is used in **time expressions** . . .

    1. **to indicate the amount of time spent doing (or not doing) something.** The action of the verb takes place either **some time during the** (a) or **over the entire** (b) **time period given**. **Note** that in this construction, Russian does not use a preposition to translate the English preposition "for." (p. 37)

        a. Они́ рабо́тали там неде́лю. They worked there **for a week**.

        b. Мы живём в Москве́ год (**#**).
We have been living in Moscow **for a year**.

    2. with **ка́ждый** (every), **весь** (all), and **це́лый** (whole, entire). (p. 37)

        a. Я чита́ю по-ру́сски **ка́ждый** день (**#**). I read Russian **every day**.
        b. Они́ занима́лись **всю** ночь (**#**). They studied **all night**.
        c. Она́ рабо́тает **це́лую** неде́лю. She has been working **an entire week**.

3. to express **on a particular day of the week** after the preposition **в** (p. 38).

    a. У меня́ бу́дет уро́к **в** сре́ду. I will have a lesson **on Wednesday.**

    b. Мой друг приезжа́ет **в** суббо́ту. My friend is arriving **on Saturday.**

4. to express "**at**" **a given hour** after the preposition **в**. The number is in accusative case, but the word for "o'clock" (час) is in **genitive singular after 2, 3,** and **4** and in **genitive plural after 5–12**. "At one o'clock" is rendered as "**в час**" (in accusative case without the special modifier оди́н). (**See** the chapter "Clock Time," section I, B, in this grammar for more information.) (pp. 38, 42)

                      accusative   gen. pl.

    a. Уро́к начина́ется **в** де́сять (**#**) часо́в.
    The lesson begins **at ten** o'clock.

                            acc.

    b. Я бу́ду игра́ть в те́ннис **в час** (**#**). I'm playing tennis **at one.**

5. to indicate the **frequency of an action**. The noun denoting the time element is preceded by a numeral or an indefinite numeral (ско́лько, не́сколько, мно́го), the proper form of the word **раз** (time), and the preposition **в**. (p. 38)

    a. Я говорю́ по-ру́сски три ра́за **в** неде́лю.
    I speak Russian three times **per week.**

    b. Я е́зжу в Росси́ю мно́го раз **в** год (**#**).
    I go to Russia many times **a year.**

6. to express the period of time **preceding** the occurrence of an action using the preposition **че́рез** (p. 43).

    a. Они́ прие́дут **че́рез** ме́сяц (#). They will arrive **in a month.**

    b. Заня́тия начина́ются **че́рез** неде́лю. Classes begin **in a week.**

7. to express the **duration** of the result of an action after **на** (pp. 355, 364).

    a. Мы е́дем в Росси́ю **на** неде́лю. We are going to Russia **for a week.**

                      acc. gen. sg.

    b. Я иду́ в бассе́йн **на два́** часа́. I'm going to the pool **for two** hours.

8. to express **the time needed to achieve the result of an action** (use a **perfective** verb + **за** + **accusative case**). (p. 355)

    a. Це́рковь постро́или **за́** год (#). They built the church **in a year.**

    b. Я напишу́ докла́д **за** неде́лю. I'll write the report **in a week.**

D. is used with the following **prepositions: в, на, че́рез, за, под, про.**

    1. **в, на**

        a. **Time**

            1'. **on a day of the week** = **в** + accusative (II, C, 3, above)

2'. **clock time on the hour** = **в** + accusative (II, C, 4, above)

3'. **frequency of action** = **в** + accusative (II, C, 5, above)

4'. **duration** of the result of an action = **на** + accusative (II, C, 7, above)

b. Destination of **motion** = **в/на** + accusative (II, A, above)

2. **че́рез**

a. **Time:** Time **preceding** the Occurrence of an Action (II, C, 6, above)

b. **Motion: over**, **across**, or **through** (pp. 235, 355)

1'. Они́ прошли́ **че́рез** парк (**#**).
They walked **through the park**.

2'. Тури́сты перешли́ **че́рез** у́лицу.
The tourists walked **across the street**.

3'. Самолёт летéл **че́рез** Чёрное мо́ре.
The plane flew **over (across) the Black Sea**.

3. **за** (behind)

a. **Time:** the time needed to **achieve the result of an action** = **a perfective** verb + **за** + accusative (II, C, 8, above)

b. **Motion: Destination of Motion** (p. 119)

1'. Го́сти се́ли **за** стол (**#**). The guests sat down **at the table**.

2'. Я положи́ла письмо́ **за** кни́ги.
I put the letter **behind the books**.

4. **под** (beneath, underneath): **Destination of Motion** (p. 119)

Я положи́ла письмо́ **под** кни́гу.
I put the letter **underneath the book**.

5. **про** (about): In informal Russian про кого́/что = о ком/чём (p. 156).

a. Мы говори́м **про** Ма́шу. We are talking **about Masha**.

b. Они́ мне ужé сказа́ли **про** э́то. They already told me **about that**.

E. To Express **Quantity**

1. For information on how to use **cardinal numerals** in accusative case, **see** the chapter "Cardinal Numerals," sections I–III, in this grammar.

2. For information on how to use **indefinite numerals** (ско́лько, не́сколько, мно́го, немно́го, ма́ло) in accusative case, **see** the chapter "Review: The Declension of Numerals," section IX, in this grammar.

Роди́тельный паде́ж—Genitive Case

I. Оконча́ния—Endings

A. Существи́тельные—Nouns (pp. 22, 90–92)

Endings

Падежи́ Cases	Мужско́й и сре́дний род		Же́нский и мужско́й род	Же́нский и сре́дний род		Множ. число́ м./ж. ср.	
Имени́тельный Nominative	-#	-о	-а	-#	-а	-ы	-а
Вини́тельный Accusative	Inanimate = Nom. Animate = Gen.		-у	Like Nominative		Inanimate = Nom. Animate = Gen.	
Роди́тельный Genitive	**-а**		**-ы**	**-и**		**-#/-ей/-ов**	
Предло́жный Prepositional	-е/-и[1]		-е/-и[1]	-и		-ах	
Да́тельный Dative	-у		-е/-и[1]	-и		-ам	
Твори́тельный Instrumental	-ом		-ой	-ью	-ом	-ами	

Examples

Мужско́й и сре́дний род	Жен. и муж. род	Же́нский и сре́дний род	Мно́жественное число́ муж./жен. сре́дний	
-а	**-ы**	**-и**	**-#/-ов/-ей**	
стола́			столо́в	
дня			дней	
учи́теля			учителе́й	
ножа́			ноже́й	
отца́			отцо́в	
	окна́			о́кон
	мо́ря			море́й
	зда́ния			зда́ний
	сестры́		сестёр	
	пе́сни		пе́сен	
	кни́ги		книг	
	пе́нсии		пе́нсий	
	дя́ди (м.)		дя́дей	
		две́ри	двере́й	
		и́мени		имён

---

[1] Nouns ending in **-ий**, **-ие**, or **-ия** take the ending **-и** in these cases; other nouns take the ending **-е**.

Образова́ние роди́тельного падежа́ мно́жественного числа́—Formation of the Genitive Plural (pp. 90–91)

If Nominative Singular Ends in a Vowel: -#		If Nominative Singular Ends in ж, ч, ш, щ, or ь: -ей		If Nominative Singular Ends in Hard Consonant (other than a husher) or й: -ов	
кни́га	→ книг	гара́ж	→ гаражей	дом	→ домо́в
неде́ля	→ неде́ль	дочь	→ дочере́й	парк	→ па́рков
письмо́	→ пи́сем	каранда́ш	→ карандашей	отец	→ отцо́в
ме́сто	→ мест	това́рищ	→ това́рищей	ме́сяц	→ ме́сяцев
и́мя	→ имён	писа́тель	→ писа́телей	музе́й	→ музе́ев
		дверь	→ двере́й	бой	→ боёв

-ий stems[2]

зда́ние	→ зда́ний
ле́кция	→ ле́кций

Исключе́ния—Exceptions (pp. 91–92)

Nominative Singular	Nominative Plural	Genitive Plural	Nominative Singular	Nominative Plural	Genitive Plural
друг	друзья́	друзе́й	сосе́д	сосе́ди	сосе́дей
сын	сыновья́	сынове́й	мо́ре	моря́	море́й
муж	мужья́	муже́й	по́ле	поля́	поле́й
брат	бра́тья	бра́тьев	дя́дя	дя́ди	дя́дей
стул	сту́лья	сту́льев	тётя	тёти	тётей
челове́к	лю́ди	люде́й			
ребёнок	де́ти	дете́й			

Бе́глые гла́сные—Fill Vowels (pp. 92–93)

The purpose of fill vowels is to break up a consonant cluster that is difficult to pronounce. They are inserted into the stem of a word when it has a zero ending (#). For masculine words this occurs in the nominative singular of nouns (отец), in the short form of adjectives (дово́лен), and in the special modifier чей, while for feminine and neuter words this occurs in the **genitive plural** of nouns (америка́нок, о́кон). **Remember** the following rules for fill vowels:

1. If the consonant cluster contains a velar (**к, г, х**), the fill vowel is -**o**- unless it follows a husher (**ж, ч, ш, щ**) or **й**, in which case spelling rule 2 applies and unstressed **o** → **e**.

Nom. Singular		Gen. Plural	Nom. Singular		Gen. Plural
остано́вка	→	остано́вок	де́вушка	→	де́вушек
ку́хня	→	ку́хонь[3]	де́вочка	→	де́вочек
окно́	→	о́кон	копе́йка	→	копе́ек[4]

2. Otherwise, the fill vowel is -**e**- (-**ё**- if stressed before a hard consonant). A soft sign (**ь**) in the middle of the consonant cluster is replaced with -**e**-.

---

[2] **Remember** that neuter nouns like зда́ние and feminine nouns like ле́кция have stems ending in -ий (зда́ний -о; ле́кций -а), just like the masculine noun ге́ний. For a review of this problem, see the heading "Nouns: How to Handle Stems and Endings," page 4, in this grammar.

[3] A final soft "н" becomes hard when a fill vowel is inserted before it (пе́сня → пе́сен). Notable exceptions include ку́хня → ку́хонь and дере́вня → дереве́нь.

[4] **Remember** that the **й** is not written here because of spelling rule 3. **See** the chapter "The Vowel Chart and Hard vs. Soft Consonants / Spelling Rules," section II, C, in this grammar for a more detailed explanation.

Nom. Singular		Gen. Plural	Nom. Singular		Gen. Plural
письмо́	→	пи́**сем**	дере́вня	→	дере́**вень**[5]
де́**ньги**	→	де́**нег**	статья́	→	стате́**й**[5, 6]
се**стра́**	→	сест**ёр**	семья́	→	семе́**й**[5, 6]

B. Прилага́тельные—Adjectives (pp. 64, 94)

Endings

Падежи́ Cases	Мужско́й и сре́дний род		Же́нский род	Мно́жественное число́
Имени́тельный Nominative	-ый/-о́й[7]	-ое	-ая	-ые
Вини́тельный Accusative	Inanimate = Nom. Animate = Gen.		-ую	Inanimate = Nom. Animate = Gen.
Роди́тельный Genitive	**-ОГО**		**-ОЙ**	**-ЫХ**
Предло́жный Prepositional	-ОМ		-ОЙ	-ЫХ
Да́тельный Dative	-ОМУ		-ОЙ	-ЫМ
Твори́тельный Instrumental	-ЫМ		-ОЙ	-ЫМИ

Examples

	Мужско́й и сре́дний род	Же́нский род	Мно́жественное число́
Stem	**-ОГО**	**-ОЙ**	**-ЫХ**
Hard Stems	но́вого	но́вой	но́вых
Soft Stems	си́него	си́ней	си́них
к, г, х Stems	плохо́го	плохо́й	плохи́х
ж, ч, ш, щ Stems	хоро́шего	хоро́шей	хоро́ших

C. Местоиме́ния-прилага́тельные—Special Modifiers (pp. 64, 94)

мой (твой, свой)	моего́	мое́й	мои́х
наш (ваш)	на́шего	на́шей	на́ших
весь	всего́	всей	всех
э́тот	э́того	э́той	э́тих
тот	того́	той	тех
чей	чьего́	чьей	чьих
оди́н	одного́	одно́й	одни́х

---

[5] Note that even though the fill vowel is stressed, it is written here as "e" rather than "ё" because it comes before a **soft** consonant.

[6] The stems of these nouns end in й: статъ#й -а́, семь#й -а́. The fill vowel is inserted before the **й**, thus the genitive plural ending of both nouns is -#. (A **#** in the **stem** of a word holds the place for a fill vowel.)

[7] When the ending is stressed, the masculine nominative singular adjective ending is -о́й, otherwise it is -ый.

II. Употребле́ния роди́тельного падежа́—The Uses of Genitive Case

Genitive case . . .

A. answers the question **Отку́да?** with the prepositions **из, с,** and **от** to designate the person(s) whose office or residence is the origin of motion.[8]

1. Use **из** + genitive with nouns and pronouns that use **в** to answer the questions **Куда́?** and **Где?** (pp. 21–22, 65)

a. Она́ взяла́ кни́гу **из стола́.** = She took the book **from/out of the desk.**
b. Они́ иду́т **из шко́лы.** = They are coming **from school.**

2. Use **с** + genitive with nouns and pronouns that use **на** to answer the questions **Куда́?** and **Где?** (**See** the chapter "Accusative Case," section II, A, in this grammar.) (pp. 21–22, 65)

a. Они́ иду́т **с уро́ка.** = They are coming **from the lesson.**
b. Он возвраща́ется **с ле́кции.** = He is returning **from the lecture.**

3. Use **от** with **people** to answer the questions **Отку́да? От кого́?** (pp. 35, 65)

a. Мы пришли́ **от Ива́на.** = We have come **from Ivan's (place).**
b. Я иду́ **от О́льги.** = I am coming **from Olga's (place).**

B. answers the question **Где?** or **У кого́?** with people using **у** + genitive (p. 35).

1. **У кого́** он живёт? Он живёт **у ба́бушки.**
Where is he living? He is living **at his grandmother's/with his grandmother.**

2. **Где** ты была́? Я была́ на консульта́ции **у профе́ссора Ма́ркова.**
Where were you? I was **at Professor Markov's** office hour.

Note the correspondences between prepositions. The prepositions for going "to/in(to)/on," being "at/in/on," and coming "from" are linked in the following way (pp. 23, 35):

	motion to **Куда́?**	*position in/at/on* **Где?**	*motion from* **Отку́да?**
For Places	**В** + ACC. **НА** + ACC.	**В** + PREP. **НА** + PREP.	**ИЗ** + GEN. **С** + GEN.
For People	**К** + DAT.	**У** + GEN.	**ОТ** + GEN.

C. is used **without prepositions . . .**

1. to express **possession.** (**Remember:** The possessor comes **after** the object possessed.) (p. 64)

a. Где маши́на Ива́на? Where is Ivan's car?
b. Э́то кни́га Лари́сы. This is Larisa's book.

---

[8] For a fuller treatment of the prepositions that govern genitive case, **see** section II, D, below.

2. to qualify other nouns ("**of**" **constructions**). (p. 64)

    a. Э́то мой но́вый уче́бник ру́сск**ого** языка́.
This is my new **Russian** textbook (textbook **of the Russian language**).

    b. Фёдоров — тре́нер на́ш**ей** кома́нд**ы**.
Fedorov is the coach **of our team**.

3. to indicate **absence** or that **something does not exist** (p. 64).

    a. Ива́**на** здесь нет. **Ivan** isn't here.
    b. В го́роде нет библиоте́к**и**. There is no **library** in the city.

4. to indicate the **date** on which something takes place (p. 45).

    a. Они́ прие́хали деся́т**ого** ию́ня. They arrived **on the tenth** of June.

    b. Футбо́льный матч бу́дет пя́т**ого** сентября́.
The soccer game will be **on the fifth** of September.

5. to indicate **the month or year when something occurs** when they are preceded by another expression of time. The year is given as an **ordinal** number.[9] (p. 45)

    a. Она́ начала́ учи́ться в Москве́ тридца́т**ого** а́вгуст**а**.
She began studying in Moscow on the thirtieth **of August**.

    b. На́ша ба́бушка умерла́ шесто́**го** ма́я две ты́сячи тре́ть**его** го́д**а**.
Our grandmother died on May 6, 200**3**.

6. after the verbs **боя́ться** and **жела́ть** (p. 64).

    a. Мы жела́ем вам счастли́в**ого** пути́.[10] Bon voyage!
    b. Я бою́сь пра́вд**ы**. I am afraid of **the truth**.

7. to express **abstract complements**—such as **мир** (peace), **поко́й** (peace and quiet), and **сча́стье** (happiness)—after the verb **хоте́ть** (p. 64).

    a. Кто не хо́чет ми́р**а**? Who doesn't want **peace**?
    b. Мы все хоти́м сча́сть**я**. We all want **happiness**.
    c. **But:** Я хочу́ кни́г**у** (acc. = specific, concrete). I want **the book**.

8. to indicate **size or color** (p. 64).

    a. Как**о́го** ро́ст**а** твой брат? **How tall** is your brother?
    b. Он сре́дн**его** ро́ст**а**. He's **medium height**.
    c. Как**о́го** цве́т**а** ко́шка? **What color** is the cat?
    d. Она́ чёрн**ого** цве́т**а** (чёрная). It's **black**.

---

[9] For a review of how dates are expressed in Russian, **see** the chapter "Expressions of Time Other than Clock Time," section VI, in this grammar.
[10] путь is the lone masculine noun in the third declension. Other nouns in this declension are feminine (like дверь) or neuter (like и́мя). For the full declension of путь, **see** the chapter "Nouns: Sample Declensions," section I, in this grammar.

9. to express the **partitive** genitive (p. 295).

    a. **Definition:** When a direct object denotes a part of a larger amount, it is rendered in the genitive case (rather than the accusative case). This is the partitive use of genitive case.

    b. **Endings:** Use regular genitive case endings, but **note** that some nouns—such as **чай**, **са́хар**, and **суп**—have the alternate partitive genitive ending **у**: ча́ю, са́хару, су́пу.

    Note: The translation of the partitive genitive into English is generally accomplished with the help of the word "some," whereas the same noun used as a direct object in accusative case is generally translated with the aid of the definite article "the." Except for the verb хоте́ть, use the partitive genitive after **perfective** verbs.

genitive	accusative
1'. Дай мне то́рт**а**.	Дай мне то́рт (**#**).
Give me **some** cake.	Give me **the** cake.

genitive	acc.
2'. Принеси́ ча́я/ча́ю.	Принеси́ ча́й (**#**).
Bring **some** tea.	Bring **the** tea.

D. is used after the following **prepositions**:

1. **от** = from (used with people, and moving away from a surface)[11]

    a. О́ля идёт **от** свое́го дру́г**а**. Olia is coming **from her friend's house**.
    b. Он получи́л письмо́ **от** сы́на. He received a letter **from his son**.
    c. Они́ отошли́ **от** зда́ния. They walked away **from the building**.

2. **из** = from [for nouns that take **в**], out of[12]

    a. Они́ возвраща́ются **из** шко́лы. They are returning **from school**.
    b. Э́та кни́га **из** Росси́и. This book is **from Russia**.
    c. Он оди́н **из** мои́х друзе́й. He is one **of my friends**.

3. **с** = from [for nouns that take **на**], off of (from the surface of), since[13]

    a. Они́ иду́т **с** ле́кции. They are coming **from the lecture**.
    b. Она́ взяла́ кни́гу **со** стола́. She took the book **from the table**.
    c. Я рабо́таю **с трёх часо́в**. I have been working **since three**.

4. **у** = at, by, near; at the place/home of; "have" constructions[14]

    a. Мы бы́ли **у** на́ш**их** друзе́й. We were **at our friends' (place/home)**.
    b. Они́ стоя́ли **у** о́зер**а**. They were standing **by/near/at the lake**.
    c. **У меня́** но́вая маши́на. **I have** a new car.

---

[11] For more information on the use of от, **see** II, A, 3, above.
[12] For more information on the use of из, **see** II, A, 1, above.
[13] For more information on the use of с, **see** II, A, 2, above.
[14] For more information on the use of у, **see** II, B, above.

5. **до** = until, up to, before (This means a fair amount of time before something occurred or will occur. "Right before" is rendered by **перед** + instrumental.) (p. 183)

    a. **До революции** Россией управлял царь.
    Before the revolution the tsar ruled Russia.

    b. Мы учились в Петербурге с сентября **до декабря**.
    We studied in Petersburg from September **to (until) December**.

    c. **But: Перед** уроком (instrumental case) они разговаривали.
    They were talking **before the lesson**.

6. **после** = after (p. 183)

    Они пришли **после** ужина. They arrived **after dinner**.

7. **без** = without (p. 65)

    Они пришли **без** Ивана. They arrived **without Ivan**.

8. **около** = near, close to, next to (both space and time); about (pp. 43, 357)

    a. Она живёт **около** церкви. She lives **near the church**.

    b. Она работает **около** часа.
    She's been working **about/close to an hour**.

9. **вместо** = instead of, in place of (p. 65)

    Мы слушали Чайковского **вместо** Баха.
    We listened to Tchaikovsky **instead of Bach**.

10. **из-за** = because of, on account of (p. 65)

    Мы ушли **из-за** шума. We left **because of the noise**.

11. **для** = for (for whose benefit, for what purpose) (p. 65)

    a. Эта книга **для** моей дочери. This book is **for my daughter**.
    b. Эта комната **для** нашего ребёнка. This room is **for our baby**.

E. **Cardinal Numerals: See** the chapter "Cardinal Numerals," sections II, III, and IV in this grammar (pp. 93, 95, 100).

F. **Indefinite Numerals** (сколько, несколько, много, немного, мало): **See** the chapter "Review: The Declension of Numerals," section IX, in this grammar (pp. 94, 95, 100).

G. **Время по часам—Clock Time:** Genitive case is used extensively in expressing clock time. **See** the chapter "Clock Time" in this grammar. (pp. 42–44, 72–74)

Предло́жный паде́ж—Prepositional Case
Ме́стный паде́ж—Locative Case

I. Оконча́ния—Endings

A. Существи́тельные—Nouns (pp. 7–8)

Endings

Падежи́ Cases	Мужско́й и сре́дний род		Же́нский и мужско́й род	Же́нский и сре́дний род		Мно́ж. число́ м./ж. ср.	
Имени́тельный Nominative	-#	-о	-а	-#	-а	-ы	-а
Вини́тельный Accusative	Inanimate = Nom. Animate = Gen.		-у	Like Nominative		Inanimate = Nom. Animate = Gen.	
Роди́тельный Genitive	-а		-ы	-и		-#/-ей/-ов	
Предло́жный **Prepositional**	**-е/-и¹**		**-е/-и¹**	**-и**		**-ах**	
Да́тельный Dative	-у		-е/-и¹	-и		-ам	
Твори́тельный Instrumental	-ом		-ой	-ью	-ом	-ами	

Examples

Мужско́й и сре́дний род		Жен. и муж. род	Же́нский и сре́дний род		Мно́жественное число́ муж./жен. сре́дний	
-е/-и		**-е/-и**	**-и**		**-ах**	
столе́					стола́х	
дне					днях	
ноже́					ножа́х	
ге́нии					ге́ниях	
отце́					отца́х	
	окне́				о́кнах	
	мо́ре				моря́х	
	зда́нии				зда́ниях	
		сестре́			сёстрах	
		пе́сне			пе́снях	
		кни́ге			кни́гах	
		пе́нсии			пе́нсиях	
		дя́де (м.)			дя́дях	
			две́ри		дверя́х	
				и́мени	имена́х	

---

¹ Nouns ending in -ий, -ие, or -ия take the ending -и in these cases; other nouns take the ending -е.

Note: The following masculine nouns take a stressed -ý ending in prepositional case after the prepositions **в** and **на** in addition to the regular ending -**е** after the preposition **о** (p. 8).

в аэропорту́	in/at the airport	**на** полу́	on the floor	**в** саду́	in the garden
на берегу́	on/at the shore	**в** раю́	in paradise	**в/на** углу́	in/on the corner
в лесу́	in the forest	**в** ряду́	in the row	**в/на** шкафу́	in/on the cupboard/closet

в году́ (in a [particular] year) is used in dates: в ты́сяча девятьсо́т се́мьдесят второ́м году́.

B. Прилага́тельные—Adjectives (p. 8)

Endings

Падежи́ Cases	Мужско́й и сре́дний род		Же́нский род	Мно́жественное число́
Имени́тельный Nominative	-ый/-о́й[2]	-ое	-ая	-ые
Вини́тельный Accusative	Inanimate = Nom. Animate = Genitive		-ую	Inanimate = Nom. Animate = Genitive
Роди́тельный Genitive	-ОГО		-ОЙ	-ЫХ
Предло́жный **Prepositional**	**-ОМ**		**-ОЙ**	**-ЫХ**
Да́тельный Dative	-ОМУ		-ОЙ	-ЫМ
Твори́тельный Instrumental	-ЫМ		-ОЙ	-ЫМИ

Examples

	Мужско́й и сре́дний род	Же́нский род	Мно́жественное число́
Stem	**-ОМ**	**-ОЙ**	**-ЫХ**
Hard Stems	но́вом	но́вой	но́вых
Soft Stems	си́нем	си́ней	си́них
к, г, х Stems	плохо́м	плохо́й	плохи́х
ж, ч, ш, щ Stems	хоро́шем	хоро́шей	хоро́ших

C. Местоиме́ния-прилага́тельные—Special Modifiers (p. 8)

мой (твой, свой)	моём	мое́й	мои́х
наш (ваш)	на́шем	на́шей	на́ших
весь	всём	всей	всех
э́тот	э́том	э́той	э́тих
тот	том	той	тех
чей	чьём	чьей	чьих
оди́н	одно́м	одно́й	одни́х

---

[2] When the ending is stressed, the masculine nominative singular adjective ending is -о́й, otherwise it is -ый.

II. Употребле́ния предло́жного падежа́—The Uses of Prepositional Case

Prepositional case . . .

A. answers the question **Где?** with the prepositions **в** and **на**.

Note: Nouns using **в** in accusative case use **в** in prepositional case, and nouns using **на** in accusative case use **на** in prepositional case.

Они́ иду́т **на** рабо́ту. = They are going **to** work.	Они́ **на** рабо́те. = They are **at** work.
Они́ иду́т **в** шко́лу. = They are going **to** school.	Они́ **в** шко́ле. = They are **at** school.

1. **в** = "in" or "at" (generally used with nouns denoting closed or covered spaces), and **на** = "on" (p. 9).

    a. Письмо́ **в** столе́. The letter is **in the desk**.
    b. Он рабо́тает **в** шко́ле. He is working **at school**.
    c. Кни́га лежи́т **на** столе́. The book is **on the desk**.

2. However, **на** can also mean "in" or "at" with nouns that fall into the categories noted below (p. 10). For example, Они́ бы́ли . . .

Open Spaces		**Functions and Events**	
на пло́щади	in the square	**на** (футбо́льном) ма́тче	at the (soccer) game
на стадио́не	at/in the stadium	**на** у́жине (за́втраке, обе́де)	at supper (breakfast, dinner)
на у́лице	in the street	**на** конце́рте, **на** о́пере	at the concert, at the opera
на остано́вке	at the bus stop	**на** фи́льме, **на** ле́кции	at the film, at the lecture
на ста́нции	at/in the metro station	**на** дискоте́ке	at the disco

School Terms		**Compass Points**	
на ка́федре	in the department	**на** восто́ке	in the east
на (тре́тьем) ку́рсе	(third) year in college	**на** за́паде	in the west
на факульте́те	in the department	**на** се́вере	in the north
на уро́ке	at/in the lesson	**на** ю́ге	in the south
на заня́тии	in a class		
на заня́тиях (pl.)	at/during classes; at school		
на экза́мене	at/in the exam		
на контро́льной рабо́те	at/in the test		

Seas, Oceans, Rivers, Lakes, Islands		**Certain States and Countries**	
на Чёрном мо́ре	on the Black Sea	**на** Аля́ске	in Alaska
на Ти́хом океа́не	on the Pacific Ocean	**на** Гава́йях (pl.)	in Hawaii
на Во́лге	on the Volga	**на** Ку́бе	in Cuba
на Байка́ле	on Lake Baikal	**на/в** Украи́не	in Ukraine
на Ку́бе, **на** Гава́йях (pl.)	in Cuba, in Hawaii		

And These Commonly-Used Words			
на вокза́ле	at/in the train station	**на** рабо́те	at work
на да́че	at the dacha	**на** Ура́ле	in the Ural Mountains
на заво́де	at/in the plant/factory	**на** фа́брике	at/in the factory
на Кавка́зе	in the Caucasus	**на** (тре́тьем)	on (the third) floor
на по́чте	at/in the post office	этаже́	

3. **But**, use **в** with the names for cities, states, and countries (except those noted above in II, A, 2) and the word for university (p. 9).

a. Они́ рабо́тают **в** Москве́. They are working **in Moscow**.

b. Он вы́рос в Виско́нсине. He grew up **in Wisconsin**.

c. Мы учи́лись **в** Росси́и. We were studying **in Russia**.

d. Я живу́ **в** Аме́рике. I live **in America**.

e. За́втра ру́сские фи́зики выступа́ют **в** университе́те.
The Russian physicists are speaking **at the university** tomorrow.

Note the correspondences between prepositions. The prepositions for going "to/in(to)/on," being "at/in/on," and coming "from" are linked in the following way (pp. 23, 35):

	motion to **Куда́?**	*position at/in/on* **Где?**	*motion from* **Отку́да?**
For Places	**В** + ACC. **НА** + ACC.	**В** + PREP. **НА** + PREP.	**ИЗ** + GEN. **С** + GEN.
For People	**К** + DAT.	**У** + GEN.	**ОТ** + GEN.

B. denotes **modes of transportation** (p. 196).

1. The preposition **на** + prepositional case is used to describe the means of transportation, **how one gets somewhere**. It answers the questions

На чём ты е́дешь туда́? **What** are you taking there?
or **Как** ты е́дешь туда́? **How** are you getting there?

2. Я е́ду туда́ . . .   I'm going there . . .

на авто́бусе	by bus	**на** моторо́ллере	by motor scooter
на такси́	by taxi	**на** маши́не	by car
на метро́	by subway	**на** по́езде	by train
на корабле́	by ship	**на** самолёте	by plane
на велосипе́де	by bicycle	**на** парохо́де	by steamer
на мотоци́кле	by motorcycle	**на** ло́шади	on horseback

C. denotes **being inside a closed vehicle** after the preposition **в** (p. 197).

1. **Где** вы сиде́ли?   **Where** were you sitting?

2. Мы сиде́ли. . .   We were sitting . . .

в авто́бусе	in the bus	**в** самолёте	in the plane
в такси́	in the taxi	**в** по́езде	in the train
в маши́не	in the car		

D. is used in the following **time expressions**:

    1. to express the **month** of an occurrence, use the preposition **в** (p. 45).

        a. Она́ сдала́ экза́мен **в** ма́рт**е**. She passed the exam **in March**.
        b. Её день рожде́ния **в** ноябре́. Her birthday is **in November**.

    2. to express the **year** alone, use the preposition **в** plus an **ordinal** numeral (p. 45).[3]

        a. Он роди́лся **в** ты́сяча девятьсо́т во́семьдесят пя́т**ом** год**у́**.
        He was born **in 1985**.

        b. **В** две ты́сячи четвёрт**ом** год**у́** ле́тние и́гры бы́ли в Афи́нах.
        The summer games were in Athens **in 2004**.

    3. to express the phrases **this/last/next year/semester/quarter** use the preposition **в** (p. 45).

        a. **В** бу́дущ**ем** год**у́** я пое́ду в Росси́ю. **Next year** I am going to Russia.

        b. **В** э́т**ом** семе́стр**е** у меня́ шесть ку́рсов.
        This semester I have six courses.

        c. **В** про́шл**ой** че́тверт**и** Мари́на учи́лась в Оде́ссе.
        Last quarter Marina studied in Odessa.

    4. to express **this/last/next week** use the preposition **на** (p. 46).

        a. На́ши друзья́ из Нью-Йо́рка приезжа́ют **на** э́т**ой** неде́л**е**.
        Our friends from New York are arriving **this week**.

        b. **На** про́шл**ой** неде́л**е** они́ рабо́тали ка́ждый день.
        Last week they worked every day.

E. is used after the preposition **о** (about). (p. 70)

    1. Они́ говори́ли **о** сво**ём** но́в**ом** са́д**е**.[4]
    They were talking **about their new garden**.

    2. Са́ша зна́ет **обо всём**.[5] Sasha knows **about everything**.

---

[3] To review how ordinal numerals decline, **see** the chapter "Review: The Declension of Numerals," section XIII, in this grammar (p. 372).

[4] Nouns that take the special stressed -**у́** ending in the prepositional case after **в** and **на** (such as сад → в саду́, аэропо́рт → в аэропорту́), take the regular -**е** ending after the preposition **о** (о са́де, об аэропо́рте).

[5] The preposition **о** is used before words beginning with consonants and the vowels **е, ё, ю**, and **я**. **Об** occurs before words beginning with the vowels **а, э, и, о**, and **у**. **Обо** is used before the pronoun **мне** and forms of **весь**. The most common expressions with **весь** include the neuter form **обо всём** (about everything) and the plural form **обо всех** (about everyone). (p. 70)

Да́тельный паде́ж—Dative Case

I. Оконча́ния—Endings

A. Существи́тельные—Nouns (p. 36)

Endings

Падежи́ Cases	Мужско́й и сре́дний род		Же́нский и мужско́й род	Же́нский и сре́дний род		Множ. число́ м./ж. ср.	
Имени́тельный Nominative	-#	-о	-а	-#	-а	-ы	-а
Вини́тельный Accusative	Inanimate = Nom. Animate = Gen.		-у	Like Nominative		Inanimate = Nom. Animate = Gen.	
Роди́тельный Genitive	-а		-ы	-и		-#/-ей/-ов	
Предло́жный Prepositional	-е/-и[1]		-е/-и[1]	-и		-ах	
Да́тельный Dative	**-у**		**-е/-и[1]**	**-и**		**-ам**	
Твори́тельный Instrumental	-ом		-ой	-ью	-ом	-ами	

Examples

Мужско́й и сре́дний род	Жен. и муж. род	Же́нский и сре́дний род	Мно́жественное число́ муж./жен. сре́дний	
-у	**-е/-и**	**-и**	**-ам**	
столу́			столо́м	
дню			дням	
ножу́			ножа́м	
ге́нию			ге́ниям	
отцу́			отца́м	
	окну́			о́кнам
	мо́рю			моря́м
	зда́нию			зда́ниям
	сестре́		сёстрам	
	пе́сне		пе́сням	
	кни́ге		кни́гам	
	пе́нсии		пе́нсиям	
	дя́де (м.)		дя́дям	
		две́ри	дверя́м	
		и́мени	имена́м	

---

[1] Nouns ending in -ий, -ие, or -ия take the ending -и in these cases; other nouns take the ending -е.

B. Прилага́тельные—Adjectives (p. 36)

Endings

Падежи́ Cases	Мужско́й и сре́дний род		Же́нский род	Мно́жественное число́
Имени́тельный Nominative	-ый/-о́й[2]	-ое	-ая	-ые
Вини́тельный Accusative	Inanimate = Nom. Animate = Genitive		-ую	Inanimate = Nom. Animate = Genitive
Роди́тельный Genitive	-ого		-ой	-ых
Предло́жный Prepositional	-ом		-ой	-ых
Да́тельный **Dative**	**-ому**		**-ой**	**-ым**
Твори́тельный Instrumental	-ым		-ой	-ыми

Examples

	Мужско́й и сре́дний род	Же́нский род	Мно́жественное число́
Stem	**-ому**	**-ой**	**-ым**
Hard Stems	но́вому	но́вой	но́вым
Soft Stems	си́нему	си́ней	си́ним
к, г, х Stems	плохо́му	плохо́й	плохи́м
ж, ч, ш, щ Stems	хоро́шему	хоро́шей	хоро́шим

C. Местоиме́ния-прилага́тельные—Special Modifiers (p. 36)

мой (твой, свой)	моему́	мое́й	мои́м
наш (ваш)	на́шему	на́шей	на́шим
весь	всему́	всей	всем
э́тот	э́тому	э́той	э́тим
тот	тому́	той	тем
чей	чьему́	чьей	чьим
оди́н	одному́	одно́й	одни́м

II. Употребле́ния да́тельного падежа́—The Uses of Dative Case

Dative case ...

A. answers the question **Куда́?** or **К кому́?** after the preposition **к** to express the person(s) whose office or place of residence is the object of motion (p. 35).[3]

---

[2] When the ending is stressed, the masculine nominative singular adjective ending is -о́й, otherwise it is -ый.
[3] For a fuller review of the prepositions that govern dative case, **see** sections II, H and I, below.

1. **Куда́** ты идёшь? **Where** are you going?
Я иду́ **к врачу́**. I am going **to the doctor's** (office).

2. **К кому́** они́ е́дут? **Where** are they going?
Они́ е́дут **к свое́й ма́тери**. They are going **to their mother's** (place).

Note the correspondences between prepositions. The prepositions for going "to/in(to)/on," being "at/in/on," and coming "from" are linked in the following way (pp. 23, 35):

	motion *to* **Куда́?**	position *in/at/on* **Где?**	motion *from* **Отку́да?**
For Places	**В** + ACC. **НА** + ACC.	**В** + PREP. **НА** + PREP.	**ИЗ** + GEN. **С** + GEN.
For People	**К** + DAT.	**У** + GEN.	**ОТ** + GEN.

B. denotes the **indirect object** (**to whom** or **for whom** something is done). (p. 70)

1. Роди́тели купи́ли до́чке игру́шку. The parents bought **their daughter** a toy.
2. Я напишу́ **ей** письмо́. I will write **her** a letter.

C. denotes the person whose **age** is being given (p. 142).

1. Ско́лько **ему́/ей/Ива́ну/О́льге** лет? How old is **he/she/Ivan/Olga**?

2. **Мне/тебе́/им/Никола́ю/Мари́и** два́дцать два го́да.
I/you/they/Nikolai/Maria is/are twenty-two.

D. is used for noun/pronoun complements **after the following verbs** (p. 358).

1. **звони́ть/позвони́ть** = to phone, to call

Я звони́ла А́нне. I phoned **Anna**.

2. **отвеча́ть/отве́тить** = to answer

Я отве́тил студе́нтке. I answered **the student**.

3. **помога́ть/помо́чь** = to help

Помоги́ **им**. Help **them**.

4. **сове́товать/посове́товать** = to advise

Мы сове́туем Бори́су. We are advising **Boris**.

E. is used with the verb **нра́виться/понра́виться** = to like (p. 142).

Dative case is used to express the person who is pleased; the person or thing that is liked goes into nominative case.

dative   nominative
1. **Мне** нра́вится конце́рт. **I** like the concert.

dative   nominative
2. **Ей** понра́вилась пье́са. **She** liked the play.

Remember the following distinctions between **нра́виться/понра́виться** and **люби́ть** (p. 143).

> a. Use **люби́ть** to describe a **usual or permanent attitude** toward someone or something. **Люби́ть** takes objects in the **accusative case** or **infinitives** after it.
>
> accusative
> 1'. Я люблю́ шокола́д. I like/love chocolate.
>
> accusative
> 2'. Он лю́бит свою́ жену́. He loves his wife.
>
> infinitive
> 3'. Мы лю́бим путеше́ствовать. We love to travel.
>
> b. Use **нра́виться/понра́виться** to express the **initial impression** of someone or something.
>
> 1'. Мне нра́вится твоя́ кварти́ра. I like your apartment.
>
> 2'. Я то́лько что с ним познако́мился, но мне он понра́вился. I just met him, but I like him.

F. expresses **the person who needs something** with the short form adjectives **ну́жен, нужна́, ну́жно, нужны́**. The thing or person needed is in **nominative case**, and this is the word that the form of **ну́жен**, etc., must agree with. The auxiliary verb **быть** in the past or future tense must also agree with the person or thing needed. (p. 143)

1. Что **вам** ну́жно?
What do **you** need?

2. Ива́ну нужна́ была́ кни́га.
Ivan needed the book.

3. **Мне** ну́жен (#) журна́л (#).
I need the magazine.

4. Лари́се нужны́ бу́дут газе́ты.
Larisa will need the newspapers.

G. expresses the **logical subject in impersonal constructions** with the following adverbs and verbs. **Remember** that the following constructions do not have a grammatical subject in nominative case; instead, the logical subject goes into dative case.

1. The following forms **are unchanging**. (**See** footnote 4 below, however.) They form the past tense by adding бы́ло and the future tense by adding бу́дет. (p. 143)

мо́жно = may, is permitted   **на́до/ну́жно**[4] = need to, have to, must
нельзя́ = is forbidden   **пора́** = it is time to

   a. **Мо́жно** здесь кури́ть? <u>Is</u> smoking <u>permitted</u> here?
   b. **Вам** <u>нельзя́</u> кури́ть. **You** <u>shouldn't</u> smoke.
   c. **Мне** <u>на́до бы́ло</u> занима́ться. I <u>had (needed)</u> to study.
   d. **Тебе́** <u>ну́жно бу́дет</u> занима́ться. **You** <u>will need (will have)</u> to study.
   e. **Им** <u>пора́</u> идти́. <u>It's time</u> **for them** to go.

2. The following words are frequently used in impersonal constructions (p. 143):

интере́сно = interested   **ве́село** = cheerful, enjoy oneself
тру́дно = difficult   **ску́чно** = boring
удо́бно = comfortable   **хо́лодно** = cold
жа́рко = hot   **прия́тно** = pleasant, nice

   a. **Мне** <u>интере́сно</u> знать, отку́да он?
   I <u>would like</u> to know (<u>am interested</u> in knowing) where he's from.

   b. **Ни́не** <u>ску́чно бы́ло</u> на вечери́нке. **Nina** <u>was bored</u> at the party.

   c. **Им** <u>прия́тно бу́дет</u> поговори́ть с тобо́й.
   They <u>will enjoy</u> (<u>find it pleasant</u>) talking with you.

3. The following verbs are used in impersonal constructions only in their third-person singular (neuter) forms (p. 142).

хоте́ться (хо́чется/хоте́лось)
захоте́ться (захо́чется/захоте́лось) = to feel like

приходи́ться (прихо́дится/приходи́лось)
прийти́сь (придётся/пришло́сь) = had to

   a. **Ива́ну** <u>хо́чется</u> идти́ на пляж. **Ivan** <u>feels like</u> going to the beach.

   b. **Нам** <u>пришло́сь</u> купи́ть но́вую маши́ну.
   We <u>had</u> (<u>were forced</u>) to buy a new car.

4. The following **negative constructions** are unchanging forms. The **logical subject** goes in dative case. They show tense by adding бы́ло (for past tense) and бу́дет (for future tense). They may be followed by infinitives. (p. 144)

не́когда = there is no time   **не́чего** = there is nothing
не́где = there is nowhere (location)   **не́куда** = there is nowhere (motion)

   a. **Нам** <u>не́когда</u> идти́ на пляж.
   We <u>don't have the time</u> to go to the beach.

   b. **Ему́** <u>не́чего бы́ло</u> сказа́ть. **He** <u>had nothing</u> to say.

---

[4] Like the other words in this list, **ну́жно** is an unchanging form when it is followed by an infinitive. Unlike the other words in this list, however, it functions as a short-form adjective, and thus changes form to reflect gender and number, when what is **needed** is a noun or pronoun (person or thing). **See** section II, F, above.

     c. **Им** <u>не́где бу́дет</u> игра́ть. **They** <u>will have nowhere</u> to play.
     d. **Мне** <u>не́куда</u> идти́. **I** <u>have nowhere</u> to go.

     e. **But** to express the opposite, use **есть**.

        1'. **Мне** <u>есть</u> что де́лать! **I** <u>have</u> lots to do!
        2'. **Мне** <u>есть</u> куда́ идти́.   **I'**<u>ve got</u> somewhere to go.

H. is used after the preposition к

  1. to answer the questions **Куда́?** or **К Кому́?** for **animate nouns** in order to indicate the person(s) whose office or place of residence is **the destination of motion** (p. 35).

     a. Мы идём **к** врачу́. We are going **to the doctor's (office)**.
     b. Они́ пошли́ **к** О́льге. They went **to Olga's (house/apartment/place)**.

  2. to indicate **direction** after the verbs пройти́/прое́хать when the destination is a building (rather than an open space).[5] (p. 233)

     a. Как пройти́ **к** библиоте́к**е**? How do you get **to the library**?

     b. **But:** Как прое́хать в центр (#)/на пло́щадь (#)?
     How do you get downtown/to the square? (open spaces: в/на + accusative)

  3. in conjunction with the following verbs (p. 359):

     a. **привыка́ть/привы́кнуть к** = to get used to, to get acclimated to

        Они́ привы́кли **к** пого́д**е**. They got used **to the weather**.

     b. **гото́виться/подгото́виться к** = to prepare for

        Студе́нты гото́вились **к** контро́льн**ой** в библиоте́ке.
        The students prepared **for the test** in the library.

  4. in conjunction with the short form adjective **гото́в (гото́ва, гото́вы) к** = to be prepared for (p. 359).

     Она́ гото́ва **к** контро́льн**ой**. She is prepared **for the test**.

I. is used after the preposition по, which has many meanings (according to, along, around, about, on, by), depending on context,

  1. to express **a recurring time period** (days of the week, parts of the day). Nouns are in dative **plural**. (pp. 31, 144)

     a. **по** понеде́льник**ам**, сре́д**ам** и пя́тниц**ам** =
     on Mondays, Wednesdays, and Fridays

     b. **по** утр**а́м**, **по** вечер**а́м** = mornings, evenings

---

[5] **See** the chapter "Prefixed Verbs of Motion," section II, B, 3, in this grammar for more information.

2. to express a **means of communication** (p. 144).

    a. **по** телеви́зору = **on** television   d. **по** по́чт**е** = **by** mail
    b. **по** ра́дио = **on** the radio   e. **по** фа́ксу = **by** fax
    c. **по** телефо́ну = **on the/by** phone

3. to designate an area in which there is **random motion** (p. 144).

    a. Он ходи́л **по** ко́мнат**е**. He walked **around the room**.
    b. Она́ е́здила **по** Росси́**и**. She traveled **around/in Russia**.

4. to designate **a subject** that is being studied or in which a test is being given (pp. 31, 360).

    a. курс **по** ру́сск**ой** исто́ри**и** = a course **in Russian history**
    b. контро́льная рабо́та **по** ру́сск**ому** язык**у́** = a **Russian** exam

5. to express a kind of **sporting competition**, **tournament**, or **championship**; also to designate **a champion** in a particular sport (p. 315).

    a. соревнова́ние **по** бе́г**у** = a **running** competition (a race)
    b. турни́р **по** го́льф**у** = a **golf** tournament
    c. чемпиона́т **по** баскетбо́л**у** = a **basketball** championship
    d. Он чемпио́н ми́ра **по** ша́хмат**ам**. = He is the world **chess** champion.

6. to denote the **source of a film** (p. 327).

    a. фильм **по** рома́н**у** Достое́вского = a film **from a novel** by Dostoevsky
    b. фильм **по** расска́з**у** Толсто́го = a film **based on a story** by Tolstoy

7. in these expressions (p. 145).

    a. **по** оши́бк**е** = by mistake
    b. сосе́д/сосе́дка **по** ко́мнат**е** = roommate
    c. **по** мо**ему́** мне́ни**ю** (**по-мо́ему**) = in my opinion (according to me)

Твори́тельный паде́ж—Instrumental Case

I. Оконча́ния—Endings

A. Существи́тельные—Nouns (p. 117)

Endings

Падежи́ Cases	Мужско́й и сре́дний род		Же́нский и мужско́й род	Же́нский и сре́дний род		Множ. число́ м./ж. ср.	
Имени́тельный Nominative	-#	-о	-а	-#	-а	-ы	-а
Вини́тельный Accusative	Inanimate = Nom. Animate = Gen.		-у	Like Nominative		Inanimate = Nom. Animate = Gen.	
Роди́тельный Genitive	-а		-ы	-и		-#/-ей/-ов	
Предло́жный Prepositional	-е/-и[1]		-е/-и[1]	-и		-ах	
Да́тельный Dative	-у		-е/-и[1]	-и		-ам	
Твори́тельный **Instrumental**	**-ОМ**		**-ОЙ**	**-ЬЮ**	**-ОМ**	**-АМИ**	

Examples

Мужско́й и сре́дний род	Жен. и муж. род	Же́нский и сре́дний род		Мно́жественное число́ муж./жен. сре́дний	
-ОМ	**-ОЙ**	**-ЬЮ**	**-ОМ**	**-АМИ**	
столо́м				стола́ми	
днём				дня́ми	
ножо́м				ножа́ми	
ге́нием				ге́ниями	
отцо́м				отца́ми	
	окно́м				о́кнами
	мо́рем				моря́ми
	зда́нием				зда́ниями
	сестро́й			сёстрами	
	пе́сней			пе́снями	
	кни́гой			кни́гами	
	пе́нсией			пе́нсиями	
	дя́дей (м.)			дя́дями	
		две́рью		дверя́ми[2]	
			и́менем	имена́ми	

---

[1] Nouns ending in -ий, -ие, or -ия take the ending **-и** in these cases; other nouns take the ending **-е**.

[2] The ending **-ьми́** is an acceptable alternative to the ending -ями for дверь (дверьми́) and ло́шадь (лошадьми́). It is the preferred ending for дочь (дочерьми́).

Note: Most instrumental sg. endings begin with an **o**, so remember spelling rule 2: **Unstressed o** should not be written after **soft consonants**, the "**hushers,**" (**ж, ч, ш, щ**), or **ц**. Instead write **e**. Stressed **ó** is spelled **ё** after a soft consonant (днём) and **o** after a husher or **ц** (ножо́м, отцо́м).

сестра́ → сестро́й	день → днём	нож → ножо́м	оте́ц → отцо́м
	мо́ре → мо́рем	да́ча → да́чей	ме́сяц → ме́сяцем
	зда́ние → зда́нием	Ма́ша → Ма́шей	

B. Прилага́тельные—Adjectives (p. 118)

Endings

Падежи́ Cases	Мужско́й и сре́дний род		Же́нский род	Мно́жественное число́
Имени́тельный Nominative	-ый/-о́й[3]	-ое	-ая	-ые
Вини́тельный Accusative	Inanimate = Nom. Animate = Gen.		-ую	Inanimate = Nom. Animate = Gen.
Роди́тельный Genitive	-ого		-ой	-ых
Предло́жный Prepositional	-ом		-ой	-ых
Да́тельный Dative	-ому		-ой	-ым
Твори́тельный **Instrumental**	**-ым**		**-ой**	**-ыми**

Examples

	Мужско́й и сре́дний род	Же́нский род	Мно́жественное число́
Stem	**-ым**	**-ой**	**-ыми**
Hard Stems	но́вым	но́вой	но́выми
Soft Stems	си́ним	си́ней	си́ними
к, г, х Stems	плохи́м	плохо́й	плохи́ми
ж, ч, ш, щ Stems	хоро́шим	хоро́шей	хоро́шими

C. Местоиме́ния-прилага́тельные—Special Modifiers (p. 118)

мой (твой, свой)	мои́м	мое́й	мои́ми
наш (ваш)	на́шим	на́шей	на́шими
весь	всем	всей	все́ми
э́тот	э́тим	э́той	э́тими
тот	тем	той	те́ми
чей	чьим	чьей	чьи́ми
оди́н	одни́м	одно́й	одни́ми

---

[3] When the ending is stressed, the masculine nominative singular adjective ending is -о́й, otherwise it is -ый.

II. Употребле́ния твори́тельного падежа́—The Uses of Instrumental Case

Instrumental case . . .

A. indicates the **instrument** used to do something (no preposition is used in Russian). (To express accompaniment using the preposition **c** plus the instrumental case, **see** section II, G, 1, below.) (p. 124)

1. Она́ пи́шет ру́чк**ой**. She is writing **with a pen**.
2. Он ест ло́жк**ой**. He is eating **with a spoon**.

B. is used after the following **verbs** (pp. 124–25):

1. **быть** (past and future tenses and infinitive)[4]

a. Она́ хо́чет быть президе́нт**ом**. She wants to be **president**.
b. Он бу́дет учи́тел**ем**. He will be **a teacher**.
c. Ко́мната была́ просто́рн**ой**. The room was **spacious**.

d. **But** predicates denoting **nationality** are in **nominative case** after the **past tense** of быть.

1'. Она́ была́ ру́сск**ая**. She was **Russian**.

2'. Моя́ мать была́ америка́нк**а**, а оте́ц был францу́з (#). My mother was **American**, but my father was **French**.

e. **And** remember that predicates after the **present tense** of быть, which is not expressed, are in the **nominative case**.

1'. Кто он (#)? Он био́лог (#). Who is **he**? (What does he do?) He is **a biologist**.

2'. Ли́дия Никола́евна — медсестра́, а её муж — учён**ый**. Lidia Nikolaevna is **a nurse**, and her husband is **a scientist**.

2. **станови́ться/стать** = to become **явля́ться** = generally translated the same as the verb "to be"

a. На́дя ста́нет журнали́стк**ой**. Nadia will become **a journalist**.

b. Пётр Петро́вич стал архите́ктор**ом**. Peter Petrovich has become **an architect**.

c. Она́ явля́ется президе́нт**ом** компа́нии. She is **president** of the company.

3. **рабо́тать** = to work as

a. **Кем** он рабо́тает? **What** does he do?
b. Он рабо́тает строи́тел**ем**. He is (works as) **a construction worker**.

---

[4] For more information on predicates, **see** the chapter "Sentence Structure," section I, B, in this grammar.

4. **интересова́ться/заинтересова́ться** = to be interested in

    a. Они́ <u>интересу́ются</u> биоло́гией. They <u>are interested in</u> **biology**.
    b. Мы <u>интересова́лись</u> кино́. We <u>were interested in</u> **film**.

5. **боле́ть/заболе́ть** = to be sick/ill (with) (p. 360)

    a. Он заболе́л гри́пп**ом**. He caught **the flu**. (pf. = he is still sick)
    b. Он боле́л гри́пп**ом**. He had **the flu**. (impf. = he is no longer sick)

6. **занима́ться** = to be occupied with; to study, to do homework

    a. **Чем** ты <u>занима́ешься</u>? **What** <u>are</u> you <u>up to</u> (doing) right now?
    b. Я игра́ю в ша́хматы с бра́том. I'm playing chess with my brother.

    c. Вы <u>занима́етесь</u> спо́рт**ом**? Do you <u>go in for</u> any **sports**?
    d. Мы лю́бим игра́ть в баскетбо́л. We like to play basketball.

    e. **Чем** ты <u>занима́лся</u>? **What** <u>were</u> you <u>studying</u> (<u>working on</u>)?
    f. Я <u>занима́лся</u> матема́тик**ой**. I <u>was studying</u> (<u>working on</u>) **math**.

C. is used with the following **verbs** after the preposition **с** (p. 125):

1. **говори́ть/поговори́ть с кем** = to talk with someone

    Мы уже́ говори́ли **с ним**. We already talked **with him**.

2. **знако́миться/познако́миться с кем** =
to get to know, meet (get acquainted with) someone

    Мы познако́мились **с на́шими сосе́дями**.
    We got to know **our neighbors**.

3. **знако́мить/познако́мить кого́ с кем** =
to introduce (to acquaint) one person to (with) another

    Мы познако́мили Ива́на **с О́льгой**. We introduced Ivan **to Olga**.

4. **здоро́ваться/поздоро́ваться с кем** = to greet, to say "hello" to someone

    Они́ поздоро́вались **с учи́телем**. They greeted **their teacher**.

5. **поздравля́ть/поздра́вить кого́ с чем** =
to congratulate someone on something

    Я поздравля́ю тебя́ **с Но́вым го́дом**. **Happy New Year!**

6. **проща́ться/попроща́ться (прости́ться) с кем** =
to say goodbye to someone

    Ива́н попроща́лся **с О́льгой**. Ivan said goodbye **to Olga**.

7. **случа́ться/случи́ться с кем** = to happen to (person is in instr. case)

  Что **с ней** случи́лось? What happened **to her**?

D. is used with the following **verbs** after the prepositions **над** or **за** (pp. 125–26):

  1. **рабо́тать над чем** = to work on something

   Они́ рабо́тают **над** сочине́н**ием**. They are working **on the composition**.

  2. **смея́ться/засмея́ться над кем/чем** = to laugh at someone/something

   Они́ смея́лись **над** пье́с**ой**. They were laughing **at the play**.

  3. **ду́мать над** = to think about

   Над чем ты ду́маешь всё вре́мя?
   What are you thinking **about** all the time?

  4. **a verb of motion + за кем/чем** = to get, pick up, or fetch someone/something

   a. Мы пое́хали в аэропо́рт **за А́нн**ой.
   We went to the airport **to get/pick up Anna**.

   b. Я иду́ на у́гол **за** газе́т**ой**. I am going to the corner **for a newspaper**.

E. is used with the short-form adjective **дово́лен/дово́льна/дово́льны** = satisfied (p. 117).

  1. Я о́чень дово́лен мо́**ими** студе́нт**ами**. I am very satisfied **with my students**.
  2. Они́ дово́льны свое́**й** кварти́р**ой**. They are satisfied **with their apartment**.

F. is used with the following **short-form adjectives** after the preposition **с** (p. 125):

  1. **знако́м/знако́ма/знако́мы с кем/чем** = familiar with someone/something

   Мы **с ней** знако́мы. We are acquainted **with her**.

  2. **согла́сен/согла́сна/согла́сны с кем/чем** = agree with someone/something

   Я согла́сна **с** э́т**ими** студе́нт**ами**. I agree **with these students**.

G. is used after these **prepositions: с, за, пе́ред, над, под, ме́жду,** and **ря́дом с.**

  1. **с** = to show **accompaniment** (pp. 116, 125)
  (To express the use of an object as an instrument, Russians use instrumental case without the preposition **с**. **See** section II, A, above.)

   a. Я люблю́ ко́фе **с** молоко́**м**. I like coffee **with milk**.

   b. Ва́ня **с** удово́льстви**ем** помога́л мне.
   Vania was pleased to help me (helped me **with pleasure**).

c. **And** remember how Russians state **compound subjects**.

> 1'. <u>Мы **с Ива́ном**</u> должны́ пойти́ к роди́телям.
> <u>**Ivan and I**</u> should go see our parents.

> 2'. <u>Мы **с друзья́ми**</u> собира́емся в цирк.
> <u>**My friends and I**</u> are going to the circus.

> 3'. <u>Мы **с ней**</u> рабо́таем над докла́дом.
> <u>**She and I**</u> are working on a report.

2. You can answer the question **Где?** with the following prepositions (p. 118):

a. **за** = behind, beyond

> 1'. **Где** ваш дом? **Where** is your house?
> 2'. Наш дом **за** це́рковью. Our house is **behind the church**.

b. **пе́ред** = in front of (space), before (time)

> 1'. in front of (**где?**)

>> a'. **Где** вы стоя́ли? **Where** were you standing?

>> b'. Мы стоя́ли **пе́ред** зда́нием.
>> We were standing **in front of the building**.

> 2'. before (**когда́?**) (p. 183)

>> a'. **Когда́** ты её ви́дела? **When** did you see her?
>> b'. Я ви́дела её **пе́ред** заня́тием. I saw her **before class**.

c. **над** = above

> 1'. **Где** висе́ла карти́на? **Where** was the picture hanging?

> 2'. Карти́на висе́ла **над** дива́ном.
> The picture was hanging **above the couch**.

d. **под** = below, under

> 1'. **Где** письмо́? **Where** is the letter?
> 2'. Письмо́ лежи́т **под** кни́гой. The letter is **under the book**.

e. **ме́жду** = between

> 1'. **Где** был И́горь? **Where** was Igor?

> 2'. Он сиде́л **ме́жду** Ива́ном и О́льгой.
> He was sitting **between Ivan and Olga**.

f. **ря́дом с** = next to

> 1'. **Где** вы живёте? **Where** do you live?

2'. Мы живём **ря́дом с** Петро́в**ыми**.
We live **next to the Petrovs**.

3. You can answer the question **Куда́?** with a verb expressing motion plus these prepositions (p. 118):

a. **пе́ред** = in front of

1'. **Куда́** она́ положи́ла письмо́? **Where** did she put the letter?

2'. Она́ положи́ла письмо́ **пе́ред** зе́ркал**ом**.
She put the letter **in front of the mirror**.

b. **над** = above

1'. **Куда́** он пове́сил карти́ну? **Where** did he hang the picture?

2'. Он пове́сил карти́ну **над** дива́н**ом**.
He hung the picture **above the couch**.

Note: за and **под** take accusative case after them when used with a **verb that expresses motion** (p. 119).

c. **за** = behind, beyond

1'. **Куда́** они́ пошли́? **Where** did they go?
2'. Они́ пошли́ **за** фа́брик**у**. They walked **behind the factory**.
3'. Мы се́ли **за** стол (**#**). We sat down **at the table**.

d. **под** = under, underneath

1'. **Куда́** ты положи́ла письмо́? **Where** did you put the letter?

2'. Я положи́ла письмо́ **под** кни́г**у**.
I put the letter **under(neath) the book**.

Note the correspondences among prepositions (p. 119):

Куда́ они́ се́ли?	**Где** они́ сиде́ли?	**Отку́да** они́ вста́ли?
Where did they sit down?	Where were they sitting?	From where did they get up?
ЗА + Accusative	**ЗА + Instrumental**	**ИЗ-ЗА + Genitive**
Они́ се́ли **за стол**.	Они́ сиде́ли **за столо́м**.	Они́ вста́ли **из-за стола́**.
They sat down **at the table**.	They were sitting **at the table**.	They got up **from the table**.

Куда́ он положи́л письмо́?	**Где** письмо́?	**Отку́да** он взял письмо́?
Where did he put the letter?	Where is the letter?	Where did he get the letter?
ПОД + Accusative	**ПОД + Instrumental**	**ИЗ-ПОД + Genitive**
Он положи́л письмо́ **под кни́гу**.	Письмо́ лежи́т **под кни́гой**.	Он взял письмо́ **из-под кни́ги**.
He put the letter **under the book**.	The letter is **under the book**.	He took the letter **from under the book**.

4. **Remember** these helpful phrases that use prepositions governing the instrumental case (pp. 118–19).

a. **под** = near, not far from (a city)

    1'. Они́ живу́т **под** Москво́й. They live **near Moscow**.

    2'. А́нна Ахма́това родила́сь **под** Оде́ссой.
    Anna Akhmatova was born **near Odessa**.

b. **за столо́м** = **at the table**

    Все сиде́ли **за столо́м**. Everyone was sitting **at the table**.

c. **за́ го́родом**[5] (instrumental case with a verb expressing location)
   за́ го́род[5] (accusative case with a verb expressing motion)

= out of town, in/to the country, in/to the suburbs

    1'. Мы живём **за́** го́род**ом**.
    We live **outside of town** (**in the country**).

    2'. В суббо́ту мы с жено́й пое́дем **за́ го́род**.
    On Saturday my wife and I are going **out of town** (**to the country**).

d. **за грани́цей** (instrumental case with a verb expressing location)
   за грани́цу (accusative case with a verb expressing motion)
   из-за грани́цы (genitive case after the preposition **из-за**)

= abroad

    1'. Моя́ тётя Мари́я живёт **за** грани́ц**ей**.
    My Aunt Maria lives **abroad**.

    2'. Ле́том они́ е́дут **за** грани́цу.
    They are going **abroad** this summer.

    3'. Брат Лари́сы верну́лся **из-за** грани́цы.
    Larisa's brother has returned **from abroad**.

---

[5] **Note** *the stress on the preposition* **за́**. In this phrase, the noun **го́род/ом** has no independent stress.

Склоне́ние существи́тельных: приме́ры
Nouns: Sample Declensions

I. Masculine Nouns (pp. 347, 350, 351–52)

	Singular	Plural	Singular	Plural	Singular	Plural
Stem Type:	**Hard**		**Soft**		**-ц**	
Nominative	стол (#)	столы́	день (#)	дни	оте́ц (#)	отцы́
Accusative	стол (#)	столы́	день (#)	дни	отца́	отцо́в
Genitive	стола́	столо́в	дня	дней	отца́	отцо́в
Prepositional	столе́	стола́х	дне	дня́х	отце́	отца́х
Dative	столу́	стола́м	дню	дня́м	отцу́	отца́м
Instrumental	столо́м	стола́ми	днём	дня́ми	отцо́м	отца́ми

	Singular	Plural	Singular	Plural	Singular	Plural
Stem Type:	**Velar (к, г, х)**		**Husher (ж, ч, ш, щ)**		**-ий**	
Nominative	парк (#)	па́рки	гара́ж (#)	гаражи́	ге́ний (#)	ге́нии
Accusative	парк (#)	па́рки	гара́ж (#)	гаражи́	ге́ния	ге́ниев
Genitive	па́рка	па́рков	гаража́	гараже́й	ге́ния	ге́ниев
Prepositional	па́рке	па́рках	гараже́	гаража́х	ге́нии	ге́ниях
Dative	па́рку	па́ркам	гаражу́	гаража́м	ге́нию	ге́ниям
Instrumental	па́рком	па́рками	гаражо́м	гаража́ми	ге́нием	ге́ниями

	Singular	Plural	Singular	Plural
Stem Type:	**-анин/-янин**			
Nominative	англича́нин (#)	англича́не	киевля́нин (#)	киевля́не
Accusative	англича́нина	англича́н (#)	киевля́нина	киевля́н (#)
Genitive	англича́нина	англича́н (#)	киевля́нина	киевля́н (#)
Prepositional	англича́нине	англича́нах	киевля́нине	киевля́нах
Dative	англича́нину	англича́нам	киевля́нину	киевля́нам
Instrumental	англича́нином	англича́нами	киевля́нином	киевля́нами

Masculine nouns ending in **-анин/-янин** drop the -ин suffix in the plural. They take a **-е** ending in the nominative plural and a zero (#) ending in the genitive plural. The suffix -ан/-ян denotes members of an ethnic or social group. Other nouns in this category include горожа́нин (city dweller), граждани́н (citizen), дворяни́н (nobleman), крестья́нин (peasant), христиани́н (Christian), мусульма́нин (Muslim), северя́нин (northerner), славяни́н (Slav), and южа́нин (southerner).

	Singular	Plural	Singular	Plural
Stem Type:	**-онок/-ёнок**			
Nominative	медвежо́нок (#)	медвежа́та	котёнок (#)	котя́та
Accusative	медвежо́нка	медвежа́т (#)	котёнка	котя́т (#)
Genitive	медвежо́нка	медвежа́т (#)	котёнка	котя́т (#)
Prepositional	медвежо́нке	медвежа́тах	котёнке	котя́тах
Dative	медвежо́нку	медвежа́там	котёнку	котя́там
Instrumental	медвежо́нком	медвежа́тами	котёнком	котя́тами

Masculine nouns ending in **-онок/-ёнок** denote young animals or persons. The plural forms of these nouns replace -онок/-ёнок with **-ят**. The nominative plural ending is **-a**, and the genitive plural ending is zero (#). Other nouns in this category include волчóнок (wolf cub), жеребёнок (colt), мышóнок (young mouse), слонёнок (elephant calf), and тигрёнок (tiger cub). **Remember** that the noun **ребёнок** has the standard plural form **дéти**. The plural noun ребя́та means "fellows," "guys," "lads."

	Singular	Plural	Singular	Plural
The Nouns	господи́н	**and**	хозя́ин	
Nominative	господи́н (#)	господа́	хозя́ин (#)	хозя́ева
Accusative	господи́на	госпóд (#)	хозя́ина	хозя́ев (#)
Genitive	господи́на	госпóд (#)	хозя́ина	хозя́ев (#)
Prepositional	господи́не	господа́х	хозя́ине	хозя́евах
Dative	господи́ну	господа́м	хозя́ину	хозя́евам
Instrumental	господи́ном	господа́ми	хозя́ином	хозя́евами

These two nouns drop the -ин suffix in the plural. Their feminine equivalents are госпожá and хозя́йка. Дáмы и господá = Ladies and Gentlemen.

	Singular	Plural
The Noun	путь is masculine but declines like a дверь-type noun.	
Nominative	путь (#)	пути́
Accusative	путь (#)	пути́
Genitive	пути́	путéй
Prepositional	пути́	путя́х
Dative	пути́	путя́м
Instrumental	путём	путя́ми

II. Neuter Nouns (pp. 347, 350)

	Singular	Plural	Singular	Plural	Singular	Plural
Stem Type:	**Hard**		**Soft**		**-ий**	
Nominative	окнó	óкна	мóре	моря́	здáние	здáния
Accusative	окнó	óкна	мóре	моря́	здáние	здáния
Genitive	окнá	óкон (#)	мóря	морéй	здáния	здáний (#)
Prepositional	окнé	óкнах	мóре	моря́х	здáнии	здáниях
Dative	окну́	óкнам	мóрю	моря́м	здáнию	здáниям
Instrumental	окнóм	óкнами	мóрем	моря́ми	здáнием	здáниями

	Singular	Plural	Singular	Plural
Stem Type:	**и́мя-type**			
Nominative	и́мя	именá	врéмя	временá
Accusative	и́мя	именá	врéмя	временá
Genitive	и́мени	имён (#)	врéмени	времён (#)
Prepositional	и́мени	именáх	врéмени	временáх
Dative	и́мени	именáм	врéмени	временáм
Instrumental	и́менем	именáми	врéменем	временáми

и́мя-type nouns in Russian add the suffix -ен- in every case except the nominative and accusative singular. **Note** that this noun has a hard stem in the plural (it takes "hard" endings). All nouns ending in -мя are neuter and decline like и́мя. Nouns ending in -мья (семья́), however, are feminine and decline like a second-declension noun (пéсня).

III. Feminine Nouns (pp. 347, 350)

	Singular	Plural	Singular	Plural	Singular	Plural
Stem Type:	**Hard**		**Soft**		**-ц**	
Nominative	сестра́	сёстры	пéсня	пéсни	пти́ца	пти́цы
Accusative	сестру́	сестёр (#)	пéсню	пéсни	пти́цу	пти́ц (#)
Genitive	сестры́	сестёр (#)	пéсни	пéсен (#)	пти́цы	пти́ц (#)
Prepositional	сестрé	сёстрах	пéсне	пéснях	пти́це	пти́цах
Dative	сестрé	сёстрам	пéсне	пéсням	пти́це	пти́цам
Instrumental	сестрóй	сёстрами	пéсней	пéснями	пти́цей	пти́цами

	Singular	Plural	Singular	Plural	Singular	Plural
Stem Type:	**Velar (к, г, х)**		**Husher (ж, ч, ш, щ)**		**-ий**	
Nominative	наýка	наýки	душа́	дýши	пéнсия	пéнсии
Accusative	наýку	наýки	дýшу	дýши	пéнсию	пéнсии
Genitive	наýки	наýк (#)	души́	душ (#)	пéнсии	пéнсий (#)
Prepositional	наýке	наýках	душé	дýшах	пéнсии	пéнсиях
Dative	наýке	наýкам	душé	дýшам	пéнсии	пéнсиям
Instrumental	наýкой	наýками	душóй	дýшами	пéнсией	пéнсиями

	Singular	Plural	Singular	Plural
Stem Type:	**дверь-type**		**мать/дочь**	
Nominative	дверь (#)	двéри	мать (#)	ма́тери
Accusative	дверь (#)	двéри	мать (#)	матерéй
Genitive	двéри	дверéй	ма́тери	матерéй
Prepositional	двéри	дверя́х	ма́тери	матеря́х
Dative	двéри	дверя́м	ма́тери	матеря́м
Instrumental	двéрью	дверя́ми	ма́терью	матеря́ми

IV. Names (pp. 69, 319, 352–53)

Russian first names (именá) and patronymics (óтчества) decline like nouns. Russian last names (фами́лии) are more complicated. Last names that have adjective endings (Толстóй, Достоéвский) decline like adjectives. However, Russian surnames ending in -ин or -ов/-ёв/ -ев have mixed declensions. Masculine surnames in -ин or -ов/-ёв/-ев decline like nouns in every case except instrumental, where they take an adjective ending (-ым). Feminine last names in –ина or -ова/-ёва/-ева decline like nouns in nominative and accusative case but take adjective endings (-ой) in all other cases. In the plural, surnames in -ин or -ов/-ёв/-ев take noun endings only in the nominative case; in all other cases they take adjective endings.

	Masculine	Feminine	Plural	Masculine	Feminine	Plural
Nominative	Пýшкин (#)	Пýшкина	Пýшкины	Ма́рков (#)	Ма́ркова	Ма́рковы
Accusative	Пýшкина	Пýшкину	Пýшкиных	Ма́ркова	Ма́ркову	Ма́рковых
Genitive	Пýшкина	Пýшкиной	Пýшкиных	Ма́ркова	Ма́рковой	Ма́рковых
Prepositional	Пýшкине	Пýшкиной	Пýшкиных	Ма́ркове	Ма́рковой	Ма́рковых
Dative	Пýшкину	Пýшкиной	Пýшкиным	Ма́ркову	Ма́рковой	Ма́рковым
Instrumental	Пýшкиным	Пýшкиной	Пýшкиными	Ма́рковым	Ма́рковой	Ма́рковыми

Remember: First names of **non-Russian** origin decline only if they end appropriately for their gender: a **consonant** for masculine names and -а or -я for feminine names. Thus, the masculine first names Бил and Рóберт decline, but Áнтони and Джо do not. Likewise, the feminine first names Ма́рта and Ба́рбара decline, but Нэ́нси and Мэ́ри do not.

Pronouns and Special Modifiers

I. Местоиме́ния—Pronouns (pp. 150, 347)

Ли́чные, возвра́тные и вопроси́тельные местоиме́ния
Personal, Reflexive, and Interrogative Pronouns

Case	Personal Pronouns[1]								Reflexive	Interrogative	
Nom.	я	ты	он	она́	оно́	мы	вы	они́	-----	кто	что
Acc.	меня́	тебя́	его́	её	его́	нас	вас	их	себя́	кого́	что
Gen.	меня́	тебя́	его́	её	его́	нас	вас	их	себя́	кого́	чего́
Prep.	мне	тебе́	нём	ней	нём	нас	вас	них	себе́	ком	чём
Dat.	мне	тебе́	ему́	ей	ему́	нам	вам	им	себе́	кому́	чему́
Instr.	мной	тобо́й	им	ей/е́ю[2]	им	на́ми	ва́ми	и́ми	собо́й	кем	чем

II. Местоиме́ния-прилага́тельные—Special Modifiers (pp. 348–49)

Note: Special modifiers use short forms in the nominative case and also in the accusative case (except when they modify **masculine or plural animate** nouns) and long forms everywhere else. As special modifiers—as opposed to personal pronouns—**его́** (his/its), **её** (her[s]/its), and **их** (their[s]) do not decline.

Case	Masc.	Neuter	Fem.	Plural	Masc.	Neuter	Fem.	Plural
Nom.	мой (#)	моё	моя́	мои́	твой (#)	твоё	твоя́	твои́
Acc.	мой/моего́	моё	мою́	мои́/мои́х	твой/твоего́	твоё	твою́	твои́/твои́х
Gen.	моего́		мое́й	мои́х	твоего́		твое́й	твои́х
Prep.	моём		мое́й	мои́х	твоём		твое́й	твои́х
Dat.	моему́		мое́й	мои́м	твоему́		твое́й	твои́м
Instr.	мои́м		мое́й	мои́ми	твои́м		твое́й	твои́ми

Case	Masc.	Neuter	Fem.	Plural	Masc.	Neuter	Fem.	Plural
Nom.	наш (#)	на́ше	на́ша	на́ши	ваш (#)	ва́ше	ва́ша	ва́ши
Acc.	наш/на́шего	на́ше	на́шу	на́ши/на́ших	ваш/ва́шего	ва́ше	ва́шу	ва́ши/ва́ших
Gen.	на́шего		на́шей	на́ших	ва́шего		ва́шей	ва́ших
Prep.	на́шем		на́шей	на́ших	ва́шем		ва́шей	ва́ших
Dat.	на́шему		на́шей	на́шим	ва́шему		ва́шей	ва́шим
Instr.	на́шим		на́шей	на́шими	ва́шим		ва́шей	ва́шими

Case	Masc.	Neuter	Fem.	Plural	Masc.	Neuter	Fem.	Plural
Nom.	чей (#)	чьё	чья	чьи	весь (#)	всё	вся	все
Acc.	чей/чьего́	чьё	чью	чьи/чьих	весь/всего́	всё	всю	все/всех
Gen.	чьего́		чьей	чьих	всего́		всей	всех
Prep.	чьём		чьей	чьих	всём		всей	всех
Dat.	чьему́		чьей	чьим	всему́		всей	всем
Instr.	чьим		чьей	чьи́ми	всем		всей	все́ми

---

[1] **Remember:** 1) The personal pronouns он, она́, and они́ can refer to both animate and inanimate nouns (p. 347); 2) any third-person **personal** pronoun not beginning with a consonant will have an **н-** added to it when it follows a **preposition**: "Я ви́жу его́," but "Я купи́л э́ту кни́гу для него́." (p. 63)

[2] **е́ю** is often used in written Russian or when not preceded by a preposition. The instrumental pronouns тобо́й and мной also have the alternate forms тобо́ю and мно́ю. (p. 116)

Case	Masc.	Neuter	Fem.	Plural	Masc.	Neuter	Fem.	Plural
Nom.	э́тот (#)	э́то	э́та	э́ти	тот (#)	то	та	те
Acc.	э́тот/э́того	э́то	э́ту	э́ти/э́тих	тот/того́	то	ту	те/тех
Gen.	э́того		э́той	э́тих	того́		той	тех
Prep.	э́том		э́той	э́тих	том		той	тех
Dat.	э́тому		э́той	э́тим	тому́		той	тем
Instr.	э́тим		э́той	э́тими	тем		той	те́ми

Case	Masc.	Neuter	Fem.	Plural
Nom.	оди́н (#)	одно́	одна́	одни́
Acc.	оди́н/одного́	одно́	одну́	одни́/одни́х
Gen.	одного́		одно́й	одни́х
Prep.	одно́м		одно́й	одни́х
Dat.	одному́		одно́й	одни́м
Instr.	одни́м		одно́й	одни́ми

III. Свой—One's Own (p. 152)

A. Declension: This special modifier declines as **мой** and **твой** do.

B. Use

   1. **Свой** may be substituted for forms of мой, твой, наш, and ваш as long as the subject (A) and the possessor (A) are the same.

         A   A   A
    a. Я говорю́ с **мои́м/со свои́м** бра́том. I am talking with **my** brother.

         A   A   A
    b. Вы писа́ли **ва́шим/свои́м** ба́бушкам.
    You wrote to **your** grandmothers.

   2. With third-person subjects (он, она́, они́), a form of свой **must be used** instead of его́, её, or их **when the subject and the possessor are the same**.

      a. **subject (A) and possessor (A) are the same**: use свой

            A   A
      1'. Они́ говоря́т со **свои́м** бра́том.
      They are talking with **their (own)** brother.

            A   A
      2'. Она́ писа́ла **свои́м** ба́бушкам.
      She wrote to **her (own)** grandmothers.

      b. **subject (A) and possessor (B) are not the same**: use его́, её, or их

            A   B   A   B
      1'. Они́ говоря́т с **их** бра́том. They are talking with **their** brother.

            A   B   A   B
      2'. Она́ писа́ла **её** ба́бушкам. She wrote to **her** grandmothers.

IV. Special Possessive Adjectives (pp. 154–55, 354)

A. Declension

Case	Masculine	Neuter	Feminine	Plural
Nom.	Са́шин (#)	Са́шино	Са́шина	Са́шины
Acc.	Са́шин/-ого	Са́шино	Са́шину	Са́шины/Са́шиных
Gen.	Са́шиного		Са́шиной	Са́шиных
Prep.	Са́шином		Са́шиной	Са́шиных
Dat.	Са́шиному		Са́шиной	Са́шиным
Instr.	Са́шиным		Са́шиной	Са́шиными

B. Formation and Use

Possessive adjectives can be formed from names and nicknames ending in -а/-я, such as Та́ня, Ве́ра, Ма́ша, Ми́тя, Са́ша, and Ва́ня. To form these adjectives, **remove** the ending (-а/-я) from the name, **add** the suffix -ин-, and then **add** the proper adjective ending. Special possessive adjectives decline just like any of the special modifiers: they use short forms in the nominative case and also in the accusative case (except when they modify **masculine or plural animate** nouns) and long forms everywhere else.

Name	Stem	Suffix	Adj. Ending	
Са́ша	Са́ш- +	-ин- +	а	= Са́шина

C. Examples

1. Э́то Са́шина сестра́, а э́то Ми́тины роди́тели.
This is **Sasha's** sister, and these are **Mitia's** parents.

2. Мы говори́м о Ве́рином па́рне. We are talking about **Vera's** boyfriend.

3. Они́ благода́рны Та́ниным де́тям. They are grateful to **Tania's** children.

Глаго́лы: спряже́ние—Verbs: Conjugation

I. First and Second Conjugation (Present/Future Endings) (pp. 11, 18)

Imperfective verbs in the present tense and perfective verbs in the future tense belong to one of two conjugation patterns. Conjugating a verb consists of combining three parts: 1) the **verb stem**, which carries the basic meaning of the verb, 2) a **conjugation marker**, which identifies the conjugation type the verb belongs to (first or second), and 3) a **person marker**, which identifies the subject of the verb (e.g., first-person singular [я] or second-person plural [вы]). The person markers for both conjugation patterns are the same.

Note: When adding either marker to the stem, there are a few rules to follow.

A. You may add opposites (a consonant to a vowel and a vowel to a consonant) but not likes. When likes come together (vowel plus vowel, consonant plus consonant), the first member of the pair (the last letter of the stem) drops. For instance, in the example below, the stem of the verb "speak" is говори́ (which ends in a vowel) and the conjugation marker is a vowel (и or а), so the и of the stem drops.

B. For first-conjugation verbs, the conjugation marker will always be **e** when it is unstressed and **ё** when it is stressed.

C. Remember the rules for handling the letter **й**. When **й** is followed by a vowel, it will **not** appear in writing. Instead, the combination of **й + vowel** will be replaced by the corresponding vowel symbol **below the line** in the vowel chart.

э	ы	а	о	у
е	и	я	ё	ю

For example, **й + у = ю**: чита́й + у = чита́ю

Пе́рвое спряже́ние—First Conjugation / Второ́е спряже́ние—Second Conjugation

Person/ Number	Stem	Conj. Marker	Person Marker	Verb Form	Stem	Conj. Marker	Person Marker	Verb Form
1st sg.	чита́й	#	у	чита́ю	говори́	#	у	говорю́
2nd sg.	чита́й	е/ё	шь	чита́ешь	говори́	и	шь	говори́шь
3rd sg.	чита́й	е/ё	т	чита́ет	говори́	и	т	говори́т
1st pl.	чита́й	е/ё	м	чита́ем	говори́	и	м	говори́м
2nd pl.	чита́й	е/ё	те	чита́ете	говори́	и	те	говори́те
3rd pl.	чита́й	у	т	чита́ют	говори́	а	т	говоря́т

II. Conjugation Subtypes

Since we learn Russian verbs by memorizing the infinitive (rather than the stem), it is not always possible to know exactly how a verb will conjugate or even which conjugation pattern it belongs to. For example, -**ать** is a common infinitive ending for Russian verbs—чита́ть, писа́ть, лежа́ть—but this ending is ambiguous: the first two verbs (чита́ть, писа́ть) belong to the first conjugation, while лежа́ть is a second-conjugation verb. **However, some infinitive endings are associated with one conjugation pattern or the other**, and you should memorize these

verb types. Below is a list of verb types in both the first and second conjugation. They are further divided into the categories of infinitive endings that indicate one conjugation pattern or the other and those that do not. **Remember:** the changes and alternations listed below apply only to the present/future conjugation of these verbs; they do not take place in the past tense.

A. First Conjugation

1. Infinitive Endings that **DO** Indicate a First-Conjugation Verb

		to show	to ask	to tell
a.	-ывать	пока́зывать	спра́шивать	расска́зывать
	-ываю	пока́зываю	спра́шиваю	расска́зываю
	-ываешь	пока́зываешь	спра́шиваешь	расска́зываешь
	-ывают	пока́зывают	спра́шивают	расска́зывают

		to give	to stand/get up	to get/be tired
b.	-ава́ть[1]	дава́ть	встава́ть	устава́ть
	-ава- → -а-	даю́	встаю́	устаю́
		даёшь	встаёшь	устаёшь
	(p. 11)	даю́т	встаю́т	устаю́т

		to advise	to dance	to feel
c.	-овать	сове́товать	танцева́ть	чу́вствовать
	-ова- → -у-	сове́тую	танцу́ю	чу́вствую
		сове́туешь	танцу́ешь	чу́вствуешь
	(p. 11)	сове́туют	танцу́ют	чу́вствуют

d. пить-type verbs (five total: бить, вить, лить, пить, шить)

		to drink	to pour	to sew
		пить	лить	шить
	(p. 365)	пью	лью	шью
		пьёшь	льёшь	шьёшь
		пьют	льют	шьют

		to cover	to open	to wash (trans.)
e.	крыть-type[2]	крыть	откры́ть	мыть
	-ы- → -о-	кро́ю	откро́ю	мо́ю
		крбешь	откро́ешь	мо́ешь
	(p. 132)	кро́ют	откро́ют	мо́ют

		to lift, raise	to understand	to receive, take
f.	prefix + -нять[3]	подня́ть	поня́ть	приня́ть
	-ня- → -ним-	подниму́	пойму́	приму́
	-ня- → -йм-	подни́мешь	поймёшь	при́мешь
	(p. 132)	подни́мут	пойму́т	при́мут

---

[1] The verb пла́вать does **not** belong to this conjugation subtype; it conjugates: пла́ваю, пла́ваешь, пла́вают.

[2] The verb плыть does **not** belong to this pattern; it conjugates like жить: живу́, живёшь, живу́т; плыву́, плывёшь, плыву́т.

[3] **All -нять verbs are perfective.** All -нять verbs with a prefix ending in a consonant (под-, об-) conjugate like подня́ть. Verbs with a prefix ending in a vowel (по-, за-) conjugate like поня́ть. The verb приня́ть is a special case: it's new stem is just -м- (rather than the -йм- that all other -нять verbs with adjectival prefixes have), and its stress pattern is like a -нять verb with a consonantal prefix.

		to return (trans.)	to rest, relax	to get used to
g.	-нуть	верну́ть	отдохну́ть	привы́кнуть
	-**ну**	верну́	отдохну́	привы́кну
	-**нешь/нёшь**	вернёшь	отдохнёшь	привы́кнешь
	-**нут**	верну́т	отдохну́т	привы́кнут
	(p. 12)			

		to go (by foot)	to carry (by foot)	to carry (by vehicle)
h.	-ти́ infinitives[4]	идти́	нести́	везти́
	end stress	иду́	несу́	везу́
		идёшь	несёшь	везёшь
		иду́т	несу́т	везу́т

		to be able to	to bake	to lie down
i.	-чь infinitives	мочь	печь	лечь
	г ⇔ ж / к ⇔ ч	могу́	пеку́	ля́гу
		мо́жешь	печёшь	ля́жешь
	(p. 12)	мо́гут	пеку́т	ля́гут

2. Other Groups of First-Conjugation Verbs You Should Know

Even though **you cannot tell from the infinitive how these verbs will conjugate,** you should remember that they form subgroups within the first conjugation.

a. **жить**-type[5] (p. 12)

to live	to swim
жить	плыть
живу́	плыву́
живёшь	плывёшь
живу́т	плыву́т

b. **ждать**-type (p. 159)

to wait	to take	to call	to fib, lie
ждать	брать	звать	врать
жду	беру́	зову́	вру
ждёшь	берёшь	зовёшь	врёшь
ждут	беру́т	зову́т	врут

c. **нача́ть/стать**-type (p. 159)

to begin	to stand/get up	to get tired
нача́ть	встать	уста́ть
начну́	вста́ну	уста́ну
начнёшь	вста́нешь	уста́нешь
начну́т	вста́нут	уста́нут

d. **класть**-type: -с- → -д- (pp. 132, 159)

to put (lay flat)	to lead (by foot)	to sit down	to steal	to fall down
класть	вести́	сесть	красть	упа́сть
кладу́	веду́	ся́ду	краду́	упаду́
кладёшь	ведёшь	ся́дешь	крадёшь	упадёшь
кладу́т	веду́т	ся́дут	краду́т	упаду́т

---

[4] All verbs with a -ти́ infinitive have end stress in all tenses except for perfective forms that are prefixed with вы́-.

[5] **Remember** that these verbs do **not** conjugate like крыть-type verbs. **See** section II, A, 1, e, above.

e. **писа́ть**-type (p. 11)

to write	to say	to look for, search	to cry	to cut/slice
писа́ть	сказа́ть	иска́ть	пла́кать	ре́зать
пишу́	скажу́	ищу́	пла́чу	ре́жу
пи́шешь	ска́жешь	и́щешь	пла́чешь	ре́жешь
пи́шут	ска́жут	и́щут	пла́чут	ре́жут

Note: There is a **consonant alternation** throughout the present/future conjugation of these verbs, and if the stress is on the ending, it moves back (to the left) one syllable in all forms except for the first-person singular (я). Verbs formed from писа́ть and -каза́ть are the most common in this group. They combine with many prefixes to form new verbs: записа́ться (to register), описа́ть (to describe), подписа́ть (to sign), and показа́ть (to show), приказа́ть (to order/command), указа́ть (to point out).

3. **One-of-a-Kind** First-Conjugation Verbs (p. 368)

to be	to go (by vehicle)	to go (by foot)	to sing
быть	е́хать	идти́	петь
бу́ду	е́ду	иду́	пою́
бу́дешь	е́дешь	идёшь	поёшь
бу́дут	е́дут	иду́т	пою́т

4. First-Conjugation Verbs with **an "-с-" before the Infinitive Ending**

a. Sometimes the -с- is part of the stem and remains in the present/future conjugation of the verb.

to carry	to grow
нести́	расти́
несу́	расту́
несёшь	растёшь
несу́т	расту́т

b. Sometimes the -с- is holding the place of another consonant that will appear in the present/future conjugation of the verb. The following group of verbs (**класть-type verbs**) form a subgroup within first conjugation that replaces the -с- of the infinitive with a -д- in the present/future conjugation (**see** section II, A, 2, d, above).

to put (lay flat)	to lead (by foot)	to sit down
класть	вести́	сесть
кладу́	веду́	ся́ду
кладёшь	ведёшь	ся́дешь
кладу́т	веду́т	ся́дут

c. **How can you tell** when the -с- will remain in the present/future conjugation and when it will be replaced by another consonant? **Look at another word that contains the same root.** If an с or a ш is in the root of the related word (and it doesn't come immediately before an infinitive ending), the -с- will remain in the present/future conjugation of the verb.

However, if a consonant other than **с** or **ш** completes the root of the related word, the -**с**- will be replaced by a different consonant in the present/future conjugation of the verb.

> 1'. не**сти́** is the unidirectional imperfective verb of motion meaning "to carry." The multidirectional imperfective verb of motion meaning "to carry" is но**си́ть**. From the verb но**си́ть** we can see that -**с**- is part of the root meaning "to carry," thus the -**с**- will stay in the conjugation of не**сти́**. We could make the same conclusion by looking at the noun подно́**с** ("tray" [an object to carry things on]).

> 2'. ве**сти́** is the unidirectional imperfective verb of motion meaning "to lead." The multidirectional pair for this verb is во**ди́ть**. From во**ди́ть** we can see that the root for "leading" ends in a **д**. In other words, the -**с**- in ве**сти́** is only holding the place of the -**д**- in the infinitive, and the -**д**- returns in the perfective/future conjugation of the verb. We could make the same conclusion by looking at the noun перево́**д** ("translation"), which is formed from the same root as во**ди́ть** and ве**сти́**.

B. **Second Conjugation** (p. 18)

1. **Multisyllabic** Verbs Ending in -**ить** indicate a Second-Conjugation Verb

to speak	to hurry	to buy
говори́ть	спеши́ть	купи́ть
говорю́	спешу́	куплю́
говори́шь	спеши́шь	ку́пишь
говоря́т	спеша́т	ку́пят

2. Second-Conjugation Verbs Ending in -**ать**

As mentioned above, infinitives ending in -**ать** constitute a very large group of verbs that **belong to both the first and second conjugations**. Most of these verbs belong to the first conjugation and conjugate like чита́ть. The number of second-conjugation verbs belonging to this category is not large. **Below is a list of second-conjugation verbs ending in -ать that you should memorize.**

to hear	to stand	to be afraid of
слы́шать	стоя́ть	боя́ться
слы́шу	стою́	бою́сь
слы́шишь	стои́шь	бои́шься
слы́шат	стоя́т	боя́тся

Also: лежа́ть (to lie [be in a prone position]), держа́ть (to keep/hold), дрожа́ть (to tremble/quiver), дыша́ть (to breathe), крича́ть (to scream), молча́ть (to be silent/quiet), стуча́ть (to knock), спа́ть [сплю, спишь, спят] (to sleep)

C. Infinitive Endings that DO NOT indicate a Certain Conjugation Pattern

	to read	to write	to lie (position)
1. -ать	чита́ть I	писа́ть I	лежа́ть II
	чита́ю	пишу́	лежу́
(pp. 11, 18)	чита́ешь	пи́шешь	лежи́шь
	чита́ют	пи́шут	лежа́т

2. multisyllabic verbs ending in -еть[6]

	to turn/become red	to see	to look/watch
	красне́ть I	ви́деть II	смотре́ть II
(p. 18)	красне́ю	ви́жу	смотрю́
	красне́ешь	ви́дишь	смо́тришь
	красне́ют	ви́дят	смо́трят

D. Irregular Verbs (p. 368)

to give	to eat	to want	to run (unidirectional)
дать	есть	хоте́ть	бежа́ть
дам	ем	хочу́	бегу́
дашь	ешь	хо́чешь	бежи́шь
даст	ест	хо́чет	бежи́т
дади́м	еди́м	хоти́м	бежи́м
дади́те	еди́те	хоти́те	бежи́те
даду́т	едя́т	хотя́т	бегу́т

III. Consonant Changes

In **some** verbs **the final consonant of the stem** changes in the present/future conjugation. Sometimes this change is predictable from the infinitive (second-conjugation verbs in -ить, first-conjugation verbs in -чь); for other verbs you must memorize when the changes occur.

A. **Consonantal Alternations in the Russian Verb:** Here is a list of the consonants that **can** undergo change in the Russian verb and the new consonant or consonant cluster that they become. Consonants that undergo this change include the dentals (**т, д, с, з**), velars (**к, г, х**), and labials (**б, п, в, м**). **Remember** that only the last consonant of the stem—спроси́ть, отве́тить, купи́ть—is eligible for this change. (p. 18)

с, х	→	ш	б	→	бл
т, к	→	ч	п	→	пл
г, з, д	→	ж	в	→	вл
ст, ск	→	щ	м	→	мл

B. **When** do these alternations occur?

1. **Second-Conjugation Verbs:** If the final consonant(s) of the stem in a second-conjugation verb is (are) from one of the two left-hand columns above, it (they) **will change** to the letter(s) in the corresponding right-hand column **in the first-**

---

[6] First-conjugation verbs with this infinitive ending conjugate like красне́ть: -ею, -еешь, -еют. The one exception is петь: пою́, поёшь, пою́т. The conjugation of second-conjugation verbs with this infinitive ending is predictable once you know that the verb belongs to the second conjugation.

person singular only. The original stem consonant(s) will return in all other forms. (p. 18)

с → ш	т → ч	д → ж	б → бл	п → пл
to ask	*to answer*	*to see*	*to love/like*	*to buy*
спроси́ть	отве́тить	ви́деть	люби́ть	купи́ть
спрошу́	отве́чу	ви́жу	люблю́	куплю́
спро́сишь	отве́тишь	ви́дишь	лю́бишь	ку́пишь
спро́сит	отве́тит	ви́дит	лю́бит	ку́пит
спро́сим	отве́тим	ви́дим	лю́бим	ку́пим
спро́сите	отве́тите	ви́дите	лю́бите	ку́пите
спро́сят	отве́тят	ви́дят	лю́бят	ку́пят

2. **First-conjugation verbs** are trickier. You can't tell which verbs undergo this change just by looking at the infinitive ending (as you can for second-conjugation verbs ending in -ить). The good news is that there are relatively few first-conjugation verbs that undergo a consonantal alternation. Also, when the final consonant of a first-conjugation verb changes, it changes (with the exception noted in section III, B, 3, below) **in all forms of the present/future conjugation**. Verbs you need to watch for include ones formed with писа́ть and -каза́ть. (p. 11)

с → ш	с → ш	з → ж	з → ж	ск → щ
to write	*to describe*	*to say/tell*	*to show*	*to look for/search*
писа́ть	описа́ть	сказа́ть	показа́ть	иска́ть
пишу́	опишу́	скажу́	покажу́	ищу́
пи́шешь	опи́шешь	ска́жешь	пока́жешь	и́щешь
пи́шет	опи́шет	ска́жет	пока́жет	и́щет
пи́шем	опи́шем	ска́жем	пока́жем	и́щем
пи́шете	опи́шете	ска́жете	пока́жете	и́щете
пи́шут	опи́шут	ска́жут	пока́жут	и́щут

3. The small class of **first-conjugation verbs with the infinitive ending** -чь provides a unique, but predictable, type of alternation. Their present/future alternation pattern is either г/ж or к/ч. In all cases, these verbs use the hard consonant (г or к) in the first-person singular (я) and the third-person plural (они́), whereas the "hushing" consonants (ж or ч) appear in all other forms.

г/ж	г/ж	к/ч	к/ч
to help	*to lie down*	*to bake*	*to flow*
помо́чь	лечь	печь	течь
помогу́	ля́гу	пеку́	
помо́жешь	ля́жешь	печёшь	
помо́жет	ля́жет	печёт	течёт
помо́жем	ля́жем	печём	
помо́жете	ля́жете	печёте	
помо́гут	ля́гут	пеку́т	теку́т

But how do you know which alternation will take place, г/ж or к/ч? If you know another word formed from the same root—it could be a verb, noun, or adjective—it will give you a clue.

помо́чь: помога́ть (the imperfective pair of помо́чь) has a **г** as the final consonant of the stem, so the alternation in помо́чь will be **г/ж**.

лечь: ложи́ться (the imperfective pair of лечь) has a **ж** as the final consonant of the stem, so the alternation in лечь will be **г/ж**.

печь: пече́нье (cookies) has a **ч** in its stem, so the alternation in печь will be **к/ч**.

течь: тече́ние (flow, current, trend) has a **ч** in its stem, so the alternation in течь will be **к/ч**.

Глаго́лы: вре́мя, ударе́ние—Verbs: Tense, Stress

I. Проше́дшее вре́мя—Past Tense

A. Оконча́ния—Endings (pp. 50–51)

In the past tense, Russian verbs do not conjugate. They agree with the subject in number, and in the singular they also agree with the subject in gender.

1. For most verbs with **the infinitve ending -ть**, simply replace the infinitive ending with the past-tense marker -л and the proper gender/number markers: -**#** (masculine), -**а** (feminine), -**о** (neuter), and -**и** (plural).[1]

    a. чита́ть: Он чита́л   Она́ чита́ла   Они́ чита́ли
    b. говори́ть: Он говори́л Она́ говори́ла Они́ говори́ли

2. Verbs with the infinitive ending -**чь** and a few verbs with the infinitive ending -**ть** and -**ти́ do not have the -л marker in the masculine past tense.** Some examples to memorize include

    a. мочь: **Он мог**   Она́ могла́   Они́ могли́
    b. печь: **Он пёк**   Она́ пекла́   Они́ пекли́
    c. лечь: **Он лёг**   Она́ легла́   Они́ легли́

    d. везти́: **Он вёз**   Она́ везла́   Они́ везли́
    e. нести́: **Он нёс**   Она́ несла́   Они́ несли́

    f. умере́ть: **Он у́мер** Она́ умерла́ Они́ у́мерли

3. A few verbs add the past tense marker -л in all forms but either drop the final consonant before the infinitive ending or use a different past-tense stem altogether. You should memorize the past tense of the following verbs:

    a. сесть: Он сел   Она́ се́ла   Они́ се́ли
    b. есть: Он ел   Она́ е́ла   Они́ е́ли
    c. вести́: Он вёл   Она́ вела́   Они́ вели́
    d. идти́:   Он шёл   Она́ шла   Они́ шли

B. Ударе́ние—Stress (pp. 51–52)

1. Most verbs have fixed stress in the past tense,

    a. рабо́тать: рабо́тал рабо́тала рабо́тали
    b. спроси́ть: спроси́л спроси́ла спроси́ли

2. **but** there are some common exceptions you should know.

    a. -**нять** verbs and **нача́ть** are stressed on the first syllable, except in the feminine form, which has end stress.

---

[1] **Remember:** кто takes masculine past-tense verbs (Кто пришёл (#)?), and что and всё take neuter (Что случи́лось? Всё бы́ло хорошо́.).

1′.	нача́ть:	на́чал	начала́	на́чали
2′.	поня́ть:	по́нял	поняла́	по́няли
3′.	заня́ть:	за́нял	заняла́	за́няли
4′.	приня́ть:	при́нял	приняла́	при́няли

b. **брать/взять, быть, дать, ждать, жить, пить,** and **спать**: the feminine ending is stressed; all other forms are stressed on the stem.

1′.	брать:	брал	брала́	бра́ли	
2′.	взять:	взял	взяла́	взя́ли	
3′.	жить:	жил	жила́	жи́ли	
4′.	быть:	был	была́	бы́ли	бы́ло
5′.	**But:**	забы́л	забы́ла	забы́ли	
6′.	**And:**	не́ был	не была́	не́ были	не́ было

c. Verbs with infinitives ending in **-чь** and **-ти́** have stress on the ending throughout the past tense.

1′.	лечь:	лёг	легла́	легли́
2′.	мочь:	мог	могла́	могли́
3′.	нести́:	нёс	несла́	несли́
4′.	вести́:	вёл	вела́	вели́

d. **роди́ться** is the only second-conjugation verb with a stress shift onto the endings of the past tense.

1′. Он роди́лся
2′. Она́ родила́сь
3′. Они́ родили́сь

II. Настоя́щее вре́мя—Present Tense

A. Спряже́ние—Conjugation (pp. 11, 18)

Present tense can only be formed from **imperfective verbs.** They conjugate according to the two patterns (**first and second conjugation**) given in section I of the chapter "Verbs: Conjugation," in this grammar.

B. Ударе́ние—Stress

In the present tense (and in the perfective future [**see** section III, B, 2, below]) there are three types of stress patterns: 1) fixed on the ending, 2) fixed on the stem, and 3) alternating, which starts on the ending in the first-person singular (я) form and then moves back (to the left) one syllable in all other forms.

1. говори́ть	2. чита́ть	3. купи́ть
говорю́	чита́ю	куплю́
говори́шь	чита́ешь	ку́пишь
говори́т	чита́ет	ку́пит
говори́м	чита́ем	ку́пим
говори́те	чита́ете	ку́пите
говоря́т	чита́ют	ку́пят

III. Бу́дущее вре́мя—Future Tense

A. Несоверше́нный вид—Imperfective Verbs (pp. 105, 129)

The future tense of imperfective verbs is formed using the auxiliary verb **быть** (я бу́ду, ты бу́дешь, он/она́ бу́дет, мы бу́дем, вы бу́дете, они́ бу́дут) **plus the imperfective infinitive**.

1. **Я бу́ду писа́ть** ка́ждый день. I **will write** every day.
2. Мы ча́сто **бу́дем** тебе́ **звони́ть**. We **will call** you often.

B. Соверше́нный вид—Perfective Verbs

1. Спряже́ние—Conjugation (pp. 11, 18, 129)

There is no special conjugation for the future tense of perfective verbs. When perfective verbs are given in their simple conjugation (**see** the chapter "Verbs: Conjugation," section I, in this grammar), they have a future meaning.

a. Она́ **ска́жет** ему́. She **will tell** him.
b. Они́ **ку́пят** маши́ну. They **will buy** the car.

2. Ударе́ние—Stress

The same stress patterns (fixed on the ending, fixed on the stem, and alternating) that apply to imperfective verbs in the present tense also apply to perfective verbs in the future tense. **See** section II, B, above.

Глаго́лы: вид—Verbs: Aspect

Russian has two aspects, **несоверше́нный вид** (imperfective aspect) and **соверше́нный вид** (perfective aspect). Aspect is an expressive grammatical concept, and much of what English communicates through a complex series of tenses, Russian expresses via aspect. **Remember:** Aspect is only a consideration in the past and future tenses in Russian; present tense can only be formed from imperfective aspect.

Perfective aspect is the more restrictive of the two aspects. Generally, perfective aspect is used when 1) an action has occurred (or will occur) **one time**, 2) a **result** has been (will be) achieved (the action has been [will be] completed), and 3) the result is **still in effect** (it has not been [will not be] reversed or annulled).

Imperfective aspect is used when the result of an action is unimportant. Instead, it stresses **the action itself** in either the past or future tenses. Adverbs and adverb phrases are used to express the duration of the action or how often it was (will be) repeated.

I. Проше́дшее вре́мя—Past Tense

A. Употребле́ние несоверше́нного ви́да—The Use of Imperfective Aspect

Remember: Imperfective aspect does not mean that an action was not completed; in most cases, however, it does not specify whether or not it was.

Imperfective aspect . . .

1. expresses action that has taken place **but whose result is not mentioned** (p. 78).

   a. Вчера́ ве́чером я смотре́ла телеви́зор. Yesterday I watched TV.

   (This expresses the idea of watching an unspecified amount of TV rather than a program from start to finish.)

   b. У́тром Бори́с игра́л в хокке́й. Boris played hockey this morning.

   (This sentence uses imperfective aspect because it emphasizes the action of the verb—Boris **played** hockey—rather than a result, such as he played a **game** of hockey.)

2. expresses **habitual/repeated** actions or actions taking place **over time** (p. 78).

   a. Она́ писа́ла письмо́ ба́бушке **ка́ждую неде́лю**.
   She wrote a letter to her grandmother **every week**.

   b. Она́ печа́тала рефера́т **два часа́**.
   She typed her paper **for two hours**.

3. expresses **simultaneous** actions (p. 78).

   a. Они́ слу́шали му́зыку и чита́ли газе́ту.
   They listened to music and read the newspaper.

b. Они́ обе́дали и разгова́ривали. They ate dinner and conversed.

4. denotes **how time was spent** earlier (prior to moment of conversation). Use imperfective for both the question and the answer. (p. 78)

 a. Что ты де́лала вчера́ ве́чером? What did you do last night?
 b. Я писа́ла дома́шнее зада́ние. I worked on (wrote) my homework.

 Note: You might have finished your homework, but imperfective aspect doesn't specify whether or not you did. In this type of question, and also the answer to it, the emphasis is on what you **did** (**how you spent your time**), not whether or not you completed it.

5. answers questions of the type: **"Have you _ever_ done this?"** Both the question and answer are imperfective. (p. 78)

 a. Вы чита́ли *Войну́ и мир*? Have you (ever) read *War and Peace*?
 b. Да. Чита́л. Yes. I have.

6. denotes **actions that can be reversed or annulled**. These verbs come in pairs of antonyms, such as брать/взять (to take) and дава́ть/дать (to give). Use of imperfective aspect denotes either that the action occurred one time but **has been reversed or annulled** or that it has occurred **more than one time** (habitual or repeated action as in section I, A, 2 above). (p. 248)

 a. Он открыва́л окно́. He opened the window. (impf. = now it's closed)
 b. Она́ заходи́ла. She dropped in. (impf. = but she's no longer here)

 But:
 c. Он откры́л окно́. He opened the window. (pf. = it's still open)
 d. Она́ зашла́. She has dropped in. (pf. = she is still here)

 Here is a list of verbs you should know from this category:

брать/взять	дава́ть/дать	to take ⇔ to give
приезжа́ть/прие́хать	уезжа́ть/уе́хать	to arrive ⇔ to depart
приходи́ть/прийти́	уходи́ть/уйти́	to come ⇔ to leave
входи́ть/войти́	выходи́ть/вы́йти	to enter ⇔ to exit
заходи́ть/зайти́	уходи́ть/уйти́	to drop in ⇔ to leave
ложи́ться/лечь	встава́ть/встать	to lie down ⇔ to get up
сади́ться/сесть	встава́ть/встать	to sit down ⇔ to get up
открыва́ть/откры́ть	закрыва́ть/закры́ть	to open ⇔ to close

7. denotes that there was **no intention** to undertake an action **when the verb is negated** (p. 79).

 a. Она́ мне **не** звони́ла. She didn't call me. (impf. = never intended to)

 b. В суббо́ту мы **не** ходи́ли в парк.
 On Saturday we didn't go to the park. (impf. = had no intention of going)

B. Употребле́ние соверше́нного ви́да—The Use of Perfective Aspect

Perfective aspect . . .

1. describes **the result of an action** (p. 78).

    a. Мы почини́ли маши́ну. We repaired the car.
(It's fixed and ready to go.)

    b. Мари́я сдала́ экза́мен. Maria passed the exam.
(She completed it successfully.)

2. refers to **an expected action** and its result. This use of perfective aspect answers the question: **"Have you done what you wanted/intended/were supposed to do?"** (p. 78)

    a. Она́ написа́ла письмо́. She wrote the letter.
    b. Мы купи́ли маши́ну. We bought a car.
    c. Я вы́мыл посу́ду. I washed the dishes.

3. denotes **consecutive/sequential actions** that happen only one time. This category includes verbs expressing an action that is completed before another action begins (a, b) or when the time of an action whose result is not reversed immediately is mentioned (c). (pp. 78, 248)

    a. Они́ пришли́ в музе́й и вошли́ в зал.
They arrived at the museum and entered the hall.

    b. Они́ сыгра́ли в ша́хматы и посмотре́ли фильм.
They played a **game** of chess and **then** watched **the film** (in its entirety).

    c. Мой друг прие́хал на ста́нцию вчера́ в семь часо́в.
My friend arrived at the station yesterday at seven o'clock.

But: If they are not completed, consecutive actions would be expressed with imperfective aspect.

    d. Они́ слу́шали му́зыку и пото́м смотре́ли телеви́зор.
They listened to music and then watched television.
(Neither verb expresses a definite result, even though they are sequential.)

4. expresses **actions that can be reversed or annulled**. Verbs expressing these types of actions come in pairs of antonyms, such as брать/взять (to take) and дава́ть/дать (to give). Use of perfective aspect denotes that **the action occurred one time and is still in effect** (it hasn't been reversed or annulled). **See** the list of verbs you should know in this category in section I, A, 6, above. (p. 248)

    a. Да. Я взял его́ кни́гу. Yes. I took his book. (pf. = I still have it.)
    b. Он дал мне свою́ кни́гу. He gave me his book. (pf. = I still have it.)

    c. **But:** Он дава́л мне кни́гу. He gave me the book.

(impf. = I no longer have it. He gave it to me, but the action has been reversed or annulled. [I gave it back or gave it to someone else.])

5. denotes that an **intended** action did not take place **when the verb is negated** (p. 79).

    a. Мы не реши́ли все зада́чи. We didn't solve all the problems.

    (We **tried**, but for some reason—we ran out of time, the problems were too difficult—we didn't solve them.)

    b. Мы не пошли́ в парк. Шёл дождь.
    We didn't go to the park. It was raining.

    (We **intended** to go, but the rain stopped us.)

II. Бу́дущее вре́мя—Future Tense

A. Употребле́ние несоверше́нного ви́да—The Use of Imperfective Aspect

Imperfective aspect . . .

1. expresses an action that will take place in the future with **no reference to a result** (p. 130).

    a. Они́ бу́дут учи́ться в Москве́. They will study in Moscow.
    b. Я бу́ду слу́шать му́зыку. I'll be listening to music.

2. expresses an action when **duration** is noted.

    a. Они́ бу́дут рабо́тать **всю** ночь. They will work **all** night.
    b. Мы бу́дем чита́ть **два часа́**. We'll read **for two hours**.

3. denotes **repeated** actions. Look for key words like **ка́ждый** or a form of **раз**.

    a. Мы бу́дем чита́ть по-ру́сски **ка́ждый день**.
    We will read Russian **every day**.

    b. Я бу́ду писа́ть домо́й **раз в неде́лю**.
    I'll write my family **once a week**.

4. expresses what someone is going to do, **how he or she will spend time**.

    a. Что ты бу́дешь де́лать?
    What are you going to do? What will you be doing?

    b. Я бу́ду рабо́тать и пото́м бу́ду отдыха́ть.
    I'll be working and then I'll relax.

    Note: Imperfective is used in these sentences because the emphasis is on how you intend to **spend time**, not on what you intend to accomplish. In this type of question and the answers to it, results are not important.

B. Употребле́ние соверше́нного ви́да—The Use of Perfective Aspect

Perfective aspect (p. 129) . . .

1. expresses a **one-time action** in the future that will produce a **result** and **does not occur over time**. These actions are often called instantaneous.

    a. Я **дам** ей э́ту кни́гу. I **will give** her this book.
    b. Она́ **придёт** в час. She **will get here** at one o'clock.

2. with the prefixes **по-** (for a short time) and **про-** (for a long time) can express an action that is **limited by time**.

    a. Мы **по**игра́ем в па́рке. We will play **for a while** in the park.
    b. Мы до́лго **про**сиди́м в кла́ссе. We'll be in class **for a long time**.

3. with the prefixes **за-** and **по-** can express the **beginning of an action**.

    a. Они́ ско́ро **за**пою́т пе́сню. They **will** soon **break out** in song.
    b. Фильм **по**йдёт в суббо́ту. The film **starts** (**will start**) on Saturday.

III. Инфинити́вы—Infinitives

A. Use **imperfective infinitives** . . .

1. after conjugated forms of **быть** to form **the future tense of imperfective verbs**. (**See** the chapter "Verbs: Tense, Stress," section III, A, in this grammar.)

    a. Я **бу́ду чита́ть** зада́ние. I'll **be reading** the assignment.

    b. Сего́дня ве́чером мы **бу́дем смотре́ть** фильм.
We **are going to be watching** a movie this evening.

2. after the verbs **хоте́ть, уме́ть, мочь, собира́ться, проси́ть**, and **сове́товать** as well as after the adverbs **на́до, ну́жно**, and **мо́жно** to denote repeated actions or action in general. (Using perfective infinitives after these verbs and adverbs denotes a one-time action. **See** section III, B, 1, below.)

    a. Мой мла́дший брат **уме́ет рабо́тать** на компью́тере.
My little brother **knows how to use** the computer.

    b. Она́ всегда́ **хо́чет приглаша́ть** то́лько свои́х друзе́й.
She always **wants to invite** only her friends.

    c. Им **мо́жно ходи́ть** в кино́ ка́ждую суббо́ту.
They **can** (**are allowed to**) go to the movies every Saturday.

3. after verbs that denote the beginning, end, or continuation of an action, such as **начина́ть/нача́ть, зака́нчивать/зако́нчить, переставáть/переста́ть**, and **продолжа́ть/продо́лжить**.

    a. Студе́нты **на́чали чита́ть**. The students **began to read**.
    b. Фе́дя **переста́л рабо́тать**. Fedia **stopped working**.

4. after **не на́до, нельзя́, не хо́чется/не хоте́лось**, and in any context that indicates an action is **not necessary or not allowed**.

> a. **Не на́до** ей **звони́ть**. You **don't need to call** her.

> b. Вам **нельзя́ брать** де́ньги.
> You **aren't allowed to accept** money.

> c. Мне **не хоте́лось зака́нчивать** курсову́ю рабо́ту.
> I **didn't feel like finishing** my term paper.

5. to express **requests, decisions, and advice NOT to do something**.

> a. Роди́тели сказа́ли мне **не покупа́ть** э́ту маши́ну.
> My parents told me **not to buy** this car.

> b. Я сове́тую тебе́ **не снима́ть** э́ту кварти́ру.
> I advise you **not to rent** this apartment.

6. after the adverb **пора́** (it's time to) to indicate that an action should be occurring.

> a. **Пора́ ложи́ться** спать. **It's time to go** to bed.

> neuter
> b. **Пора́ бы́ло идти́. It was time to go.**

B. Use **perfective infinitives** . . .

1. after the verbs **хоте́ть, уме́ть, мочь, собира́ться, проси́ть**, and **сове́товать** as well as after the adverbs **на́до, ну́жно**, and **мо́жно** to denote a one-time action. (Using imperfective infinitives after these verbs and adverbs denotes repeated actions or action in general. **See** section III, A, 2, above.)

> a. Воло́дя **хо́чет** его́ **пригласи́ть**. Volodia **wants to invite** him.

> b. Мы **собира́емся пойти́** в кино́.
> We **are going (intend to go)** to the movies.

> c. Им **на́до скопи́ровать** э́ту диске́ту.
> They **need to copy** this disk.

2. after **забы́ть, успе́ть** (to have enough time to), and **уда́ться** (to succeed in doing something).

> a. Я **забы́л вы́ключить** телеви́зор. I **forgot to turn off** the TV.

> b. Ю́лия **успе́ла зако́нчить** свою́ курсову́ю рабо́ту.
> Julia **had enough time to finish** her term paper.

> dative   neuter
> c. Мне **удало́сь купи́ть** всё, что ну́жно.
> I **managed to buy** everything I needed.

IV. Checklist of Verbal Aspect

A. **Imperfective** aspect expresses . . .

1. action when no result is mentioned (I, A, 1; II, A, 1).

2. habitual or repeated action and action over time (I, A, 2; II, A, 2 and 3).

3. simultaneous action (I, A, 3).

4. how time was spent (What did/will you do? [I, A, 4; II, A, 4]).

5. the question: **"Have you <u>ever</u> done this?"** and the answer to it (I, A, 5).

6. action that has been reversed or annulled (I, A, 6).

7. negated action that was **not** intended to take place (I, A, 7).

8. - - -

B. **Perfective** aspect expresses . . .

action that occurs one time and produces a result (I, B, 1; II, B, 1).

action that takes place over time with the prefixes **по**- (for a while) and **про**- (for a long time). (II, B, 2)

consecutive or sequential actions (I, B, 3).

- - -

an expected action ("Have you done what you **wanted/intended/were supposed** to do?" [I, B, 2]).

action that can be reversed or annulled but is still in force (has **not** been reversed or annulled [I, B, 4]).

negated action that **was** intended to take place (I, B, 5).

the completion of the beginning of an action with the prefixes **за**- (**заигра́ть** = to start playing) and **по**- (**пойти́** = to start, begin). (II, B, 3)

Verbs of Position and Placing

I. The verbs **стоя́ть**, **висе́ть**, and **лежа́ть** are used to express **position**. They are often translated as the equivalent of the English verb "to be" and are **intransitive** (do not take a direct object). (p. 113)

A. **Спряже́ние—Conjugation**

стоя́ть	висе́ть	лежа́ть
стою́		лежу́
стои́шь		лежи́шь
стои́т	виси́т	лежи́т
стои́м		лежи́м
стои́те		лежи́те
стоя́т	вися́т	лежа́т

B. **Употребле́ние—Use**

(The transitive counterparts of these verbs are placed in brackets next to the appropriate intransitive verb.)

1. **стоя́ть** = to stand (be in an upright position) [**ста́вить, поста́вить**]

 a. В углу́ **стои́т** кни́жный шкаф. The bookcase **is** in the corner.
 b. Кни́ги **стоя́т** на по́лке. The books **are** on the shelf.

2. **висе́ть** = to hang [**ве́шать, пове́сить**]

 a. Над дива́ном **виси́т** карти́на.
 The picture **is** (**hanging**) above the couch.

 b. Жаке́т **висе́л** на ве́шалке.
 The jacket **was** (**hanging**) on the coat stand.

3. **лежа́ть** = to lie (to be in a prone position) [**класть, положи́ть**]

 a. На полу́ **лежи́т** ковёр. The rug **is** on the floor.
 b. Кни́ги **лежа́т** на по́лке. The books **are** (**lying**) on the shelf.

II. The verbs **ста́вить/поста́вить**, **ве́шать/пове́сить**, and **класть/положи́ть** are used to express **putting something into position**. They are **transitive** (take a direct object). (p. 113)

A. **Спряже́ние—Conjugation**

(по-)ста́вить	ве́шать	пове́сить	класть	положи́ть
(по-)ста́влю	ве́шаю	пове́шу	кладу́	положу́
(по-)ста́вишь	ве́шаешь	пове́сишь	кладёшь	поло́жишь
(по-)ста́вят	ве́шают	пове́сят	кладу́т	поло́жат

B. Употребле́ние—Use

(The intransitive counterparts of these verbs are placed in brackets next to the appropriate transitive verb.)

1. **ста́вить, поста́вить** = to put (upright, in a standing position) [**стоя́ть**]

   a. Мы **поста́вили** ме́бель в гости́ную.
   We **put** the furniture into the living room.

   b. Я **ста́влю** кни́ги на по́лку.
   I **am putting** the books (upright) on the shelf.

2. **ве́шать, пове́сить** = to hang [**висе́ть**]

   a. А́ня **пове́сила** плака́т на сте́ну.
   Ania **hung** the poster on the wall.

   b. Я **пове́шу** жаке́т на ве́шалку.
   I **will hang** my jacket on the coat rack.

3. **класть, положи́ть** = to put (in a flat, prone, lying position) [**лежа́ть**]

   a. Мы **положи́ли** ковёр на пол.
   We **put** (**laid**) the rug on the floor.

   b. Я **кладу́** кни́ги на по́лку.
   I **am putting** (**laying**) the books on the shelf.

Verbs of Asking and Answering

I. спрáшивать/спросúть *когó о чём* or *когó/у когó, что* (pp. 101, 305)

    A. Definition: to ask **someone**, to ask **about something**, to ask **for information (with a question phrase)**

    Note: You should not use this verb with the noun вопрóс (question). Instead use задавáть/задáть вопрóс (**see** section III, below).

    B. Grammar

        1. **когó о чём**: If you are asking **about something**, the person who is asked goes into accusative case (**когó**) and the thing being asked about goes into prepositional case after the preposition **о (о чём)**. See example a, below.

        2. **когó/у когó, что**: If you are asking for **information**, the person being asked is in either genitive case after the preposition **у (у когó)** or in accusative case (**когó**). Information is asked for with a question phrase, such as **what . . .** (**что . . .**), **where . . .** (**где . . .**), or **who . . .** (**кто . . .**). See examples b and c, below.

                                    accusative   prepositional
        a. Óльга Ивáновна <u>спросúла</u> Сáшу **о вáшем нóвом дóме**.
        Olga Ivanovna <u>asked</u> **Sasha about your new house.**

                (gen.)/acc.
        b. Онú <u>спросúли</u> (**у**) **меня, что** я бýду дéлать сегóдня вéчером.
        They <u>asked</u> **me what** I was doing tonight.

                    genitive/accusative
        c. Мой друзья <u>спросúли</u> **у Лéны/Лéну, кто** э́то?
        My friends <u>asked</u> **Lena, who** that was.

II. просúть/попросúть *что/чегó у когó* or *когó + infinitive* (p. 305)

    A. Definition: to **request**, to ask **for something (a noun or pronoun)**, to ask someone **to do something (with an infinitive)**

    B. Grammar

        1. **что/чегó у когó**: If you are asking for **something**, it goes into accusative case (**что**) if it is concrete and specific (example a, below) and in genitive case (**чегó**) if it is abstract or general (example b, below). The person who is asked goes into genitive case after the preposition **у (у когó)**.

        2. **когó + infinitive**: If the subject is asking someone **to do** something, the person who is being asked goes into accusative case (**когó**) and the action is expressed with an **infinitive** (example c, below).

                    genitive accusative
a. Сын <u>попроси́л</u> **у нас** велосипе́д (**#**).
Our son <u>asked</u> **us** <u>for</u> **a bicycle**.

                genitive
b. Все <u>про́сят</u> по́мощи.
Everyone <u>is asking for</u> **help**.

           accusative   infinitive
c. Они́ <u>попро́сят</u> Ната́шу ему́ **позвони́ть**.
They <u>will ask</u> **Natasha to call** him.

III. задава́ть/зада́ть вопро́с *кому́* (p. 101)

A. Definition: "to ask a question"

Note: Use this construction in order literally to express the phrase "to ask a question."

B. Grammar

    1. The noun **вопро́с** follows the verb in accusative case (**что**).

    2. The person asked is in dative case (**кому́**).

                dative   dative accusative
    a. Я хочу́ <u>зада́ть</u> Любо́ви и И́горю <u>вопро́с</u>.
    I want <u>to ask</u> **Liubov** and **Igor** <u>a question</u>.

                  dative   accusative
    b. Профе́ссор Ма́рков <u>за́дал</u> **нам** <u>са́мые тру́дные вопро́сы</u>.
    Professor Markov <u>asked</u> **us** <u>the most difficult questions</u>.

IV. отвеча́ть/отве́тить *кому́ на что* (p. 101)

A. Definition: "to answer"

B. Grammar

    1. The person who is being answered goes in dative case (**кому́**).

    2. To answer "a question" is **на** + accusative case (**на вопро́с**).

                dative
    a. Я уже́ отве́тила мое́й сестре́. I have already answered **my sister**.

             accusative
    b. Я отве́чу **на ваш вопро́с**. I will answer **your question**.

Возврáтные констрýкции—Reflexive Constructions

I. Возврáтное местоимéние—The Reflexive Pronoun (p. 150)

A. Склонéние—Declension

Nominative	- - -
Accusative	себя́
Genitive	себя́
Prepositional	себé
Dative	себé
Instrumental	собóй

B. Употреблéние—Use

1. These pronouns always refer to and take their meaning from the subject, which is always **the same person denoted by the reflexive pronoun.**

a. Accusative
Я ви́жу **себя́** в зéркале.
I see **myself** in the mirror.

b. Genitive
Он бои́тся **себя́. He** is afraid of **himself.**

c. Prepositional
Они́ говоря́т о **себé.**
They are talking about **themselves.**

d. Dative
Онá помогáла **себé. She** helped **herself.**

e. Instrumental
Мы довóльны **собóй.**
We are satisfied with **ourselves.**

2. The Verb **чýвствовать** (p. 272) . . .

a. **uses** the reflexive pronoun **себя́** to express how the subject is feeling: well (хорошó), bad (плóхо), OK (нормáльно).

1'. Как вы **себя́** чýвствуете? How are you feeling?
2'. Я чýвствую **себя́** хорошó. I feel well/fine.

b. **does not use** the reflexive pronoun **себя́** to express that the subject **senses** something.

1'. Мать чýвствует, что Марк лю́бит меня́.
My mother feels that Mark loves me.

2'. Он чýвствует свою́ вину́. He feels his (own) guilt.

3. The constructions **к себé** (кудá?) and **у себя́** (где?) indicate the place where one is normally expected to be: at home, in one's room, at the office.

a. Онá идёт **к себé.** She is **going home/to her office.**

b. Профе́ссор Ма́рков бу́дет **у себя́** по́сле уро́ка.
Professor Markov will be **in his office** after the lesson.

II. Возвра́тные глаго́лы—Reflexive Verbs (pp. 151–52)

Note: In reflexive verbs, the direct-object pronoun is already a part of the verb (-ся is a contraction of себя́); therefore, they never take a direct object in the accusative case.

A. Some verbs occur only with the reflexive particle -ся. Know the following:

1.	боя́ться *кого́/чего́?*	to be afraid of, to fear
2.	здоро́ваться/поздоро́ваться *с кем?*	to say hello (здра́вствуйте)
3.	наде́яться *на кого́/что?*	to rely on, to count on
4.	нра́виться/понра́виться *кому́?*	to appeal to
5.	догова́риваться/договори́ться *с кем?*	to make an arrangement
6.	просыпа́ться/просну́ться	to wake up
7.	остава́ться/оста́ться	to remain, to stay behind
8.	случа́ться/случи́ться *с кем?*	to happen to
9.	смея́ться/засмея́ться *над кем?*	to laugh at
10.	улыба́ться/улыбну́ться *кому́?*	to smile at
11.	учи́ться *где?* (impf. only)	to be a student somewhere

B. The following verbs have reflexive forms only in the imperfective aspect:

1.	сади́ть**ся**/сесть	to sit down
2.	ложи́ть**ся**/лечь	to lie down
3.	станови́ть**ся**/стать	to become

C. The verb **дружи́ть/подружи́ться** (to be friends) has the reflexive particle -ся only in the perfective aspect.

D. Many **transitive verbs** (verbs that take a direct object in the accusative case) **can be made intransitive** by adding the particle -ся.

Transitive Verbs (without -ся)	**Intransitive Verbs (with -ся)**
1. *to return, to give back* **возвраща́ть/верну́ть**	*to return, to get back* **возвраща́ться/верну́ться**
2. *to meet, to run into* **встреча́ть/встре́тить**	*to meet with, to date* **встреча́ться/встре́титься**
3. *to prepare, to make ready* **гото́вить/пригото́вить**	*to prepare for, to study for,* *to get ready for* **гото́виться/пригото́виться**
4. *to introduce* **знако́мить/познако́мить**	*to meet, to get acquainted* **знако́миться/познако́миться**
5. *to collect, to gather* **собира́ть/собра́ть**	*to get together; to intend; to pack* **собира́ться/собра́ться**

Transitive Verbs (without -ся)	**Intransitive Verbs (with -ся)**

6. *to teach*
учи́ть/научи́ть

to learn how to
учи́ться/научи́ться

Note: Pay special attention to the verbs "**to begin**" and "**to end**." The transitive forms of these verbs are used only with animate subjects, and the intransitive forms are used only in the third person and with inanimate subjects.

7. *to begin*
начина́ть/нача́ть

to begin
начина́ться/нача́ться

Профе́ссор **начина́ет** уро́к.
The professor **begins** the lesson.

Уро́к **начина́ется**.
The lesson **begins**.

8. *to end*
конча́ть/ко́нчить

to end
конча́ться/ко́нчиться

Мы **ко́нчили** рабо́ту.
We have finished work.

Рабо́та **ко́нчилась**.
Work is over (finished).

E. Passive Voice

Reflexive verbs are one way to form the **passive voice** in Russian. Transitive verbs create active voice constructions, and the reflexive forms of the same verbs create passive voice constructions.

1. **Active Voice** (The agent or "doer" of the action is also the subject of the sentence.)

subject and agent
a. Профе́ссор начина́ет уро́к. The professor begins the lesson.

subject/agent
b. Ма́ша закры́ла окно́. Masha closed the window.

2. **Passive Voice** (The object of the action of the verb becomes the grammatical subject of the sentence.)

subject only
a. Уро́к начина́ет**ся** в 9:00 часо́в. The lesson begins at 9:00.

subject only
b. Магази́н закры́л**ся**. The store closed.

Императи́вы—Imperatives

As in English, imperatives in Russian are used to give commands. There are several types of imperative constructions in Russian.

I. The Second-Person (ты/вы) Imperative

This imperative has two forms: the **ты** form for addressing one person in a familiar manner (a relative, a friend, a colleague of similar age and status, a child) and the **вы** form for addressing one person in a formal manner (an adult who is not a relative, friend, or colleague of similar age and status) or more than one person.[1]

A. Образова́ние—Formation (p. 24)

Form the **imperative stem** by removing the ending from the third-person plural (они́) form of the verb.

чита́(ют)   бо(я́т)ся   по́мн(ят)   ид(у́т)   вста́н(ут)   отве́т(ят)

1. If the imperative stem **ends in a vowel**, add the ending **-й** for the **ты** form of the imperative (**-йся** for reflexive verbs) and **-йте** for the **вы** form of the imperative (**-йтесь** for reflexive verbs).

a.	чита́(ют)	чита-	→ чита́й(те)
b.	бо(я́т)ся	бо- ся	→ бо́йся(-тесь)
c.	откро́(ют)	откро-	→ откро́й(те)
d.	сове́ту(ют)	совету-	→ сове́туй(те)

2. If the imperative stem **ends in two consonants** or if it **ends in one consonant and the first-person singular (я) form of the verb is stressed on the ending**, add the ending **-и** for the **ты** form of the imperative (**-ись** for reflexive verbs) and **-ите** for the **вы** form of the imperative (**-итесь** for reflexive verbs).

a.	по́мн(ят)		помн-	→ по́мни(те)
b.	чи́ст(ят)		чист-	→ чи́сти(те)
c.	ид(у́т)	(я иду́)	ид-	→ иди́(те)
d.	пи́ш(ут)	(я пишу́)	пиш-	→ пиши́(те)
e.	ска́ж(ут)	(я скажу́)	скаж-	→ скажи́(те)

3. If the imperative stem **ends in one consonant and the first-person singular (я) form of the verb does not have end stress**, add the ending **-ь** for the **ты** form of the imperative and **-ьте** for the **вы** form of the imperative.

a.	вста́н(ут)	(я вста́ну)	встан-	→ вста́нь(те)
b.	отве́т(ят)	(я отве́чу)	ответ-	→ отве́ть(те)

4. **Exceptions:** The following verbs do not form imperatives according to the models described above, so you must memorize them.

---

[1] **See** Terence Wade, *A Comprehensive Russian Grammar* (Oxford: Blackwell, 1992) 120–121.

a. **-авать** type verbs

  1'. дава́ть   →   дава́й(те)
  2'. встава́ть   →   встава́й(те)

b. **дать, есть, пить**-type verbs (**бить, вить, лить, шить**)

  1'. дать   →   да́й(те)
  2'. есть   →   е́шь(те)
  3'. пить   →   пе́й(те) [ле́й(те), бе́й(те), etc.]

c. **(по-)éхать** → поезжа́й(те)

d. **лечь** → ля́г(те) (without a soft sign)

В. Употребле́ние ви́да—The Use of Aspect with Second-Person Imperatives (pp. 290–91)

1. **Positive** Commands

a. Use **perfective** aspect for **one-time actions** that are intended to produce **results**.

  1'. **Откро́йте** дверь. **Open** the door.
  2'. **Купи́** э́ту кни́гу. **Buy** this book.
  3'. **Напиши́** ей письмо́. **Write** her a letter.

b. Use **imperfective** aspect . . .

  1'. for **repeated** actions.

    a'. Говори́ по-ру́сски **ка́ждый день.**
    Speak Russian **every day.**

    b'. **Всегда́** покупа́й о́вощи в э́том магази́не.
    Always buy vegetables in this store.

  2'. to ask someone to **continue** an action.

    a'. **Говори́, говори́!** Я слу́шаю тебя́.
    Go ahead. I'm listening. (**Keep talking!**)

    b'. **Сиди́те! Сиди́те! Stay seated! (Don't get up!)**

  3'. for **invitations** rather than commands. You should memorize the following list of expressions that use imperatives for requests:

    a'. to invite someone to visit: **Приходи́(те)** к нам.

    b'. when opening a door and inviting someone in:

      1". **Входи́(те)**, пожа́луйста.
      2". **Заходи́(те)**, пожа́луйста.
      3". **Проходи́(те)**, пожа́луйста.

c'. when asking guests to take off a coat or hat:

Раздева́йся/Раздева́йтесь

d'. to tell someone to make himself/herself at home:

1". **Бу́дь(те)** как до́ма.
2". **Чу́вствуй(те)** себя́ как до́ма.

e'. to invite someone to sit down:

1". **Сади́(те)сь** сюда́.
2". **Сади́(те)сь** за стол.

f'. to take leave of your guests:

1". **Приходи́(те)** к нам ещё.
2". **Звони́(те).**
3". **Не забыва́й(те)** нас.

g'. if you won't see someone for a long time:

1". **Пиши́(те).**
2". **Приезжа́й(те)** скоре́е.
3". **Возвраща́йся/возвраща́йтесь** скоре́е.

2. **Negative** Commands

a. Use **imperfective** aspect . . .

1'. when you don't want someone to do something.

a'. **Не покупа́й** э́ту маши́ну. **Don't buy** this car.
b'. **Не чита́й** моё письмо́. **Don't read** my letter.

2'. When you don't want someone **to go** somewhere, use a **multidirectional** unprefixed verb of motion.

a'. **Не ходи́** туда́! **Don't go** there!
b'. **Не е́здите** в центр! **Don't go** downtown!

b. Use **perfective** aspect if you are afraid someone might do something **accidentally** or **inadvertently**. Oftentimes these commands are preceded by the word **Смотри́(те)** (Make sure/be sure you don't . . .). Some verbs that denote accidental or inadvertent actions include **заблуди́ться** (to get lost), **забы́ть** (to forget), **опозда́ть** (to be late), **ошиби́ться** (to make a mistake), **потеря́ться** (to be lost), **разби́ть** (to break [something]), **упа́сть** (to fall down).

1'. **Не забу́дь** об экза́мене! **Don't forget** about the exam!
2'. **Не потеря́йте** де́ньги! **Don't lose** your money!
3'. **Смотри́, не потеря́йся! Be sure you don't get lost!**

II. Third-Person (он/она́/они́) Imperatives: "Let him/her/them" Do Something

A. Образова́ние—Formation (p. 296)

This imperative is formed using the indeclinable word **пусть** (or **пуска́й**) and the **third-person** form of the verb, either singular or plural, depending on whom you are talking about. The person or persons you are talking about go into nominative case.

B. Вид—Aspect

1. Since this is an imperative, there is no tense involved. If you use an imperfective verb, you don't get a present-tense meaning, and if you use a perfective verb, you don't get a future-tense meaning. Both aspects translate into the same thing:

   a. **Пусть** он мне **помога́ет** (imperfective). **Let** him **help** me.
   b. **Пусть** он мне **помо́жет** (perfective). **Let** him **help** me.

2. **The difference in aspect usage** translates into the following distinction:

   a. **Imperfective aspect** means that the process denoted by the verb is stressed or that something is done repeatedly or habitually.

      1'. **Пусть она́** мне **помога́ет** (imperfective), когда́ я занима́юсь ру́сским языко́м.
      Let her help me when(ever) I am studying Russian. (repetition)

      2'. **Пусть отдыха́ют. Let them rest.** (process)

      3'. **Пусть он гото́вит.**
      Let him cook. (habitually, or right at this moment)

   b. **Perfective aspect** means that the action denoted by the verb occurs one time and will be brought to completion.

      1'. **Пусть он мне помо́жет** (perfective) э́то сде́лать.
      Let him help me do this. (one time and complete it)

      2'. **Пусть она́ пригото́вит** обе́д сего́дня.
      Let her make supper tonight. (one time and complete it)

      3'. **Пусть ку́пят** маши́ну.
      Let them buy a car. (one time and complete it)

III. First-Person Imperatives: "Let's (you and I)" Do Something (p. 297)

A. Singular vs. Polite/Plural

1. If you are speaking to one person familiarly using the pronoun **ты**, use **Дава́й**.

2. If you are speaking to more than one person or to one person using the polite form **вы**, use **Дава́йте**.

B. Вид—Aspect

1. Imperfective Verbs

a. Formation: Дава́й(те) + **Infinitive**

b. Uses

1'. to stress the **process** denoted by the verb or that the action of the verb is **repeated** or **habitual**.

a'. **Дава́йте говори́ть** то́лько по-ру́сски.
Let's speak only Russian.

(Дава́йте means you are speaking to one person politely or to more than one person; imperfective implies habitual action.)

b'. **Дава́й** всегда́ **гото́вить** обе́д вме́сте.
Let's always **prepare** dinner together.

(Дава́й means you are speaking to one person familiarly; imperfective implies repetition.)

2'. For **negative** constructions use Дава́й(те) + **не бу́дем** + an imperfective infinitive.

a'. **Дава́йте не бу́дем говори́ть** по-ру́сски.
Let's not talk in Russian.

b'. **Дава́й не бу́дем** гото́вить обе́д.
Let's not make dinner.

2. Perfective Verbs

a. Formation: Дава́й(те) + the **First-Person Plural (мы)** Form of the Verb

b. Use: A perfective verb stresses that the action denoted by the verb will **occur one time** and that you intend to **complete** it.

1'. **Дава́йте ку́пим** маши́ну.
Let's buy a car.

(Дава́йте means you are speaking to one person politely or to more than one person; perfective implies that you intend to purchase a specific car.)

2'. **Дава́й помо́жем** друг дру́гу.
Let's help each other.

(Дава́й means you are speaking to one person familiarly; perfective implies that you will help each other with something until it is solved or made right.)

C. **Verbs of Motion** are often used in the first-person plural (**мы** form) without the auxiliary words дава́й(те).

    1. **Пойдём/Пое́дем** вме́сте. **Let's go** together.
    2. **Идём./Éдем.** **Let's go./Let's get going.**

IV. Suggestions in which the Speaker(s) Volunteer(s) to do Something: "Let me (я)/us (мы)" Do That (p. 298)

A. **Singular** vs. **Polite/Plural**

    1. If you are speaking to one person familiarly with the pronoun ты, use **Дава́й**.

    2. If you are speaking **to more than one person** or **to one person** with the polite form вы, use **Дава́йте**.

B. Aspect: Perfective aspect is most common in this type of imperative because you are usually telling someone that you will do (and accomplish) something for them. **Conjugate the verb in the first-person singular or plural, depending on the subject.**

    1. **Дава́й, мы** ему́ ска́жем. **Let us** tell him.

(Дава́й means you are addressing someone as **ты**; perfective aspect means that you will tell the indirect object (ему́) something in its entirety.)

    2. **Дава́йте, я** уберу́ со стола́. **Let me** clear the table.

(Дава́йте means you are talking to one person politely or to more than one person; perfective aspect means that you will finish clearing the table.)

    3. **Дава́й, я** узна́ю, когда́ придёт по́езд.
Let me find out when the train will arrive.

(Да́вай means you are talking to one person familiarly [**ты**]; perfective aspect means that you will find out the information about the arrival of the train.)

V. Use of the Verb хоте́ть (p. 304)

A. **The Subject Wants to do Something**

    1. Definition: only **one grammatical subject is involved** (The subject is the performer of the action of both verbs—хоте́ть and the infinitive.)

    2. Structure: **subject A + хоте́ть (past/present/future) + infinitive**

            A   infinitive
        a. Я **хочу́** пригласи́ть их.
        I want to invite them. (Subject A wants to do the inviting.)

            A   infinitive
        b. Они́ **хотя́т** прийти́ в го́сти.
        They want to visit. (Subject A wants to do the visiting.)

B. **Indirect Commands**: One Subject Wants **Someone Else** to do Something

    1. Definition: **Two grammatical subjects** are involved: one subject (A) wants a second subject (B) to do something.

    2. Structure: **subj. A + хоте́ть (past/pres./fut.) + что́бы + subj. B + past tense**

                A   B   past tense
        a. Я **хочу́, что́бы** ты пригласи́ла их.
        I want you to invite them. (Subject A wants subject B to do the inviting.)
        A   B

                A   B   past tense
        b. Они́ **хотя́т, что́бы** мы пришли́ в го́сти.
        They want us to visit. (Subject A wants subject B to visit.)
          A   B

VI. Indirect Commands with the Verbs **проси́ть/попроси́ть, говори́ть/сказа́ть**, and **сове́товать/посове́товать** (p. 304)

The following two constructions are synonymous with each other.

    A. **Option 1** (This is more common in spoken Russian.)

        1. Definition: Only **one grammatical subject** is involved and the person(s) you are asking, telling, or advising to do something become the object of the verb.

        2. Structure: **subject A + verb (past/present/future) + object + infinitive**

                A   object infinitive
        a. Я **попроси́ла** их позвони́ть.
        I asked them to call.

        (Subject A has asked the direct object [them] to call.)

                A   object infinitive
        b. Мы **сове́товали** ему́ прийти́ в 6 часо́в.
        We advised him to come at 6 o'clock.

        (Subject A advised the object [him] to arrive at 6 o'clock.)

    B. **Option 2** (This structure, which is identical to the indirect command using **хоте́ть** [see section V, B, above], is more common in formal and written Russian.)

        1. Definition: **Two grammatical subjects** are involved: they are linked by the conjunction **что́бы.**

        2. Structure: **subj. A + verb (past/pres./fut.) + что́бы + subj. B + past tense**

        A   B   past tense

a. **Я попроси́ла, что́бы** они́ позвони́ли.

I asked them to call.

A   B

(Subject A has asked subject B to call.)

        A   B past tense

b. **Мы сказа́ли, что́бы** он пришёл в 6 часо́в.

We told him to come at 6 o'clock.

A   B

(Subject A has told subject B to arrive at 6 o'clock.)

Глаго́лы движе́ния без приста́вок
Unprefixed Verbs of Motion

There are fourteen unprefixed verbs of motion in Russian. In this chapter, we study the eight most common ones. The unique thing about unprefixed verbs of motion is that they have **TWO imperfective forms**, one that expresses **unidirectional motion** (movement or transportation from point "A" to point "B") and another that expresses **multidirectional motion** (generalized or habitual movement or transportation). (pp. 193–94)

I. Спряже́ние—Conjugation (p. 196)

Unidirectional Imperfectives	Multidirectional Imperfectives
идти́: иду́, идёшь, иду́т/шёл, шла (и)	ходи́ть: хожу́, хо́дишь, хо́дят/ходи́л (а, и)
е́хать: е́ду, е́дешь, е́дут/е́хал (а, и)	е́здить: е́зжу, е́здишь, е́здят/е́здил (а, и)
вести́: веду́, ведёшь, веду́т/вёл, вела́ (й)	води́ть: вожу́, во́дишь, во́дят/води́л (а, и)
везти́: везу́, везёшь, везу́т/вёз, везла́ (й)	вози́ть: вожу́, во́зишь, во́зят/вози́л (а, и)
нести́: несу́, несёшь, несу́т/нёс, несла́ (й)	носи́ть: ношу́, но́сишь, но́сят/носи́л (а, и)
лете́ть: лечу́, лети́шь, летя́т/лете́л (а, и)	лета́ть: лета́ю, лета́ешь, лета́ют/лета́л (а, и)
плыть: плыву́, плывёшь, плыву́т/плыл (а́, и)	пла́вать: пла́ваю, пла́ваешь, пла́вают/пла́вал (а, и)
бежа́ть: бегу́, бежи́шь, бегу́т/бежа́л (а, и)	бе́гать: бе́гаю, бе́гаешь, бе́гают/бе́гал (а, и)

Notes on Conjugation

A. Four of the unidirectional imperfectives are first conjugation verbs with the infinitive ending of -ти́. As such, they have end stress throughout the present and past tense and also have hard final consonants in the first-person singular (я) and third-person plural (они́) forms of the **present tense**. In the **past tense** идти́ has forms (шёл, шла, шли) that look unrelated to its present-tense conjugation, and вести́ drops the -с- of its stem. In the **masculine past tense** везти́ and нести́ do not use the marker -л.

B. When the final consonant before an infinitive ending is -с-, it sometimes is standing in for another consonant that will appear in the present/future conjugation of the verb. This is the case with вести́. The -с- is holding the place of a -д-. Thus, вести́: веду́, ведёшь, веду́т. On the other hand, in the verb нести́ the -с- is an -с- in the conjugated forms of the present tense: несу́, несёшь, несу́т. There is no way of telling whether the -с- will remain -с- in the conjugation by looking at the infinitive. You can, however, get a hint at what the consonant will be by looking at another word that uses the same root. Note that the multidirectional imperfective of нести́ is носи́ть. (The root is нос.) From this information, we can tell that the -с- in нести́ will stay. Also note that the multidirectional imperfective for вести́ is води́ть. (The root is вод.). Thus the -с- in the infinitive of вести́ will become a -д- in the conjugated forms of the verb: веду́, ведёшь, веду́т.

C. **плыть** conjugates like **жить**: живу́, живёшь, живу́т; плыву́, плывёшь, плыву́т.

D. **бежа́ть** (along with only three other verbs in Russian—дать, хоте́ть, and есть) is irregular. Its full conjugation is бегу́, бежи́шь, бежи́т, бежи́м, бежи́те, бегу́т. (p. 194)

E. Five of the eight multidirectional imperfectives are **second-conjugation verbs with infinitives ending in -ить**, and they each have a consonantal alternation (д → ж, з → ж, с → ш) in the first-person singular (я) form only. The final consonant of the stem in the infinitive comes back in all other conjugated forms.

F. Even though **пла́вать** looks like дава́ть, it does not conjugate like it. (It retains the -ва-.) дава́ть: даю́, даёшь, даю́т; пла́вать: пла́ваю, пла́ваешь, пла́вают.

II. Categorizing Imperfective Unprefixed Verbs of Motion (pp. 194–95)

A. Transitive vs. Intransitive

1. Intransitive Unprefixed Verbs of Motion
(These verbs cannot take a direct object [a noun or pronoun in accusative case] and are generally completed by prepositional phrases with the aid of such prepositions as **в, на, к, из, с,** and **от**.)

Unidirectional Motion	Multidirectional Motion	
идти́	ходи́ть	to go/come (by foot)
éхать	éздить	to go/come (by vehicle)
лете́ть	лета́ть	to fly; to go/come (by plane)
плыть	пла́вать	to swim/float/sail; to go/come (by ship)
бежа́ть	бе́гать	to run

2. Transitive Unprefixed Verbs of Motion
(These verbs take a direct object [a noun or pronoun in accusative case].)

Unidirectional Motion	Multidirectional Motion	
вести́	води́ть	to lead/take/bring (by foot)
везти́	вози́ть	to take/bring (by vehicle), to transport
нести́	носи́ть	to carry/take/bring (by foot)

B. Movement by Foot (under one's own power) vs. Movement not by Foot (using a means of conveyance)

1. Movement by Foot

a.	идти́/ходи́ть	to go/come
b.	вести́/води́ть	to lead/take/bring
c.	нести́/носи́ть	to carry/take/bring
d.	бежа́ть/бе́гать	to run

2. Movement not by Foot

a.	éхать/éздить	to go/come
b.	везти́/вози́ть	to take/carry/transport

3. лете́ть/лета́ть and плыть/пла́вать denote **motion that can be accomplished either by the subject's own power or by a means of conveyance.**

a. лете́ть/лета́ть = to fly

1'. Пти́цы летя́т на юг. The birds **are flying** south.

2'. Моя́ мать лю́бит **лета́ть** в Чика́го.
My mother likes **to fly (take the plane)** to Chicago.

b. плыть/пла́вать = to swim/float (by oneself) or to sail (by boat or ship)

> 1'. Де́ти **пла́вают** в бассе́йне.
> The children **are swimming** in the pool.

> 2'. Мы **плывём** в А́нглию. We **are sailing** (**by ship**) to England.

C. идти́/ходи́ть vs. е́хать/е́здить

1. Use **идти́/ходи́ть** when describing movement around the city or town where you live, unless you specifically mention a vehicle.

> a. Я **иду́** на конце́рт. I **am going** to the concert.

(**Note:** It is possible that you will be taking a vehicle, but since you aren't saying that you are and the motion is within your city or town, you should use a "by foot" verb. **Notice** in the following sentences that the initial destination in town is expressed with a "by foot" verb, but a vehicular verb is used to express the exact means of getting there.)

> b. Они́ **иду́т** в го́сти к дру́гу. They **are going** to visit a friend.

> c. Но как они́ **пое́дут** туда́, на метро́ и́ли на авто́бусе?
> But how **are** they **getting** there, by subway or are they taking the bus?

2. Always use **е́хать/е́здить** when referring to motion between cities or countries or to a distance that cannot be covered by foot.

> a. Ива́н **е́здил** в Москву́. Ivan **went** to Moscow.
> b. Моя́ подру́га **е́дет** в Росси́ю. My friend **is going** to Russia.

3. Use the adverb **пешко́м** with the verb идти́/ходи́ть to emphasize walking instead of riding or to contrast walking with riding.

> a. Я люблю́ **ходи́ть пешко́м**. I love **to walk**.

> b. Моя́ жена́ **е́здит** на рабо́ту, а я **хожу́ пешко́м**.
> My wife **drives** to work, but I **walk**.

III. Употребле́ние—Use

Remember that **all unprefixed verbs of motion are imperfective** and that they have the unique characteristic in Russian of having **two imperfective** forms: one denoting **unidirectional** motion, the other denoting **multidirectional** motion.

A. Unidirectional imperfectives denote **motion in one direction** (from one point to another), motion in progress toward a specific goal.

1. **Present Tense** (p. 203)

In the present tense, unidirectional imperfective verbs, such as **идти́**, **вести́**, and **е́хать**, are generally used in two ways:

a. to express the notion of "**to be on one's way**." (In this meaning they are often translated as "**to go**," "**to come**," or "**to take**".)

> 1'. Куда́ ты **идёшь**? Where **are** you **going**?
> 2'. Я **иду́** на по́чту. I **am going** to the post office.
> 3'. Я **веду́** моего́ бра́та домо́й. I **am taking** my brother home.

Note: If a destination is not named, a unidirectional verb of motion can be translated as either "**going**" or "**coming**," depending on the context (p. 206).

> Ты **идёшь** с на́ми? **Are** you **going/coming** with us?
> Вот **идёт** Ма́ша. Here **comes**/There **goes** Masha.

b. to denote **repeated motion in one direction only**.

> Я всегда́ **е́ду** на рабо́ту на авто́бусе, но домо́й я **иду́** пешко́м.
> I always **take** the bus to work, but I **walk** home.

(Even though multiple trips are implied, each verb only expresses motion in one direction: riding to work [е́хать] and walking home [идти́]. When used in this manner, unidirectional verbs have the additional meaning of "setting out for.")

2. Past and Future Tenses (p. 211)

In the past and future tenses, unidirectional imperfective verbs, such as **шёл (шла, шли)** or **бу́ду (бу́дешь,** etc.) **е́хать** are generally used in two ways:

a. to indicate **motion that was or will be in progress** when some other action occurs.

> 1'. Га́ля **шла** в магази́н, когда́ она́ уви́дела моего́ бра́та.
> Galia **was walking** to the store when she saw my brother.

> 2'. Мы **бу́дем е́хать** на конце́рт и зае́дем за Серёжей.
> **On our way** to the concert we'll pick up Seriozha.

b. to indicate **the length of an action**.

> 1'. Ско́лько вре́мени вы **е́хали** в Оде́ссу?
> How long **did it take** you **to drive** to Odessa?

> 2'. Я **бу́ду лете́ть** на Гава́йи шесть часо́в.
> It **will take me** six hours **to fly** to Hawaii.

B. Multidirectional Motion (pp. 203–204) . . .

1. denotes a **single round trip in the past tense** or a trip to a certain place and departure from it. In other words, a subject goes in one direction to go somewhere then goes in another direction to leave that place, thus the action is multidirectional.

a. Вчера́ ве́чером мы **ходи́ли** в кино́.
Yesterday evening we **went** to the movies (**and we came home**).

b. На про́шлой неде́ле они́ **е́здили** в Нью-Йо́рк.
Last week they **went** to New York. (**They are back now.**)

Note: When ходи́ть and е́здить are used in the meaning of a single round trip, they can be replaced by бы́ть with a corresponding change in case usage after the proper prepositions.

Они́ **е́здили** в Нью-Йо́рк (#). = Они́ **бы́ли** в Нью-Йо́рке.
Я **ходи́ла** на о́перу. = Я **была́** на о́пере.
Мы **ходи́ли** к друзья́м. = Мы **бы́ли** у друзе́й.

2. denotes **more than one round trip**.

a. Я ча́сто **лета́ю** в Нью-Йо́рк.
I frequently **fly** to New York. (**round trips from my home**)

b. Я **хожу́** в кино́ ка́ждую суббо́ту. I **go** to the movies every Saturday.

3. denotes **generalized or random motion** with no specific goal.

a. Ребёнок уже́ **хо́дит**. The baby **is** already **walking**.
b. Она́ **пла́вала** три ра́за в неде́лю. She **swam** three times a week.

C. Making Unprefixed Verbs of Motion Perfective with the Prefix по- (p. 224)

(**See** also the chapter "Prefixed Verbs of Motion," section II, C, 2, in this grammar.)

1. Both unidirectional and multidirectional verbs of motion can be made perfective with the prefix **по-**.

	Unidirectional	
a.	Imperfective	Perfective
1'.	идти́	пойти́
2'.	е́хать	пое́хать
3'.	лете́ть	полете́ть

	Multidirectional	
b.	Imperfective	Perfective
1'.	ходи́ть	походи́ть
2'.	е́здить	пое́здить
3'.	лета́ть	полета́ть

2. Meanings

a. Perfective verbs formed with the prefix **по-** from **unidirectional** verbs of motion **indicate the beginning of an action** in the past and future tenses. Unless there is information to the contrary, these perfectives can imply that the subject has reached or will reach his or her goal.

1'. Он **пое́хал** домо́й. He **took off/set off/started off** for home. (This verb can be used to emphasize the beginning of an action.)

OR He **went** home.

(Without information to the contrary, this verb implies he made it home.)

2'. Я **пойду́** с ва́ми в кино́. **I'll go** with you to the movies.

(This use implies that they will reach their intended goal [the movies].)

b. Perfective verbs formed with the prefix **по-** from **multidirectional** verbs of motion indicate general or random motion for **a short period of time** with no specific goal. These verbs are considered perfectives by virtue of the limit of time (to do something "for a while").

1'. Мы **походи́ли** по па́рку.
We walked around the park **for a while**.

(We didn't go to any specific destination; we just walked around [general or random motion].)

2'. Сего́дня у́тром я **попла́вала**. This morning I swam **a while**.

IV. Things to Remember

A. Indicating Modes of Transportation

1. How to say to "**take**" a bus, train, car, taxi, etc. (p. 196):

a. Use the imperative **Поезжа́й(те)** + **на** + **prepositional case**.

1'. **Поезжа́й** на метро́. **Take** the subway.
2'. **Поезжа́йте** на авто́бусе. **Take** the bus.

b. The construction **брать/взять** + **accusative case** should only be used in this meaning with **такси́** and **маши́на**. With маши́на, брать/взять can also mean "to rent a car."

1'. **Возьми́** такси́. **Take** a cab.
2'. Мы **возьмём** маши́ну в Ки́еве. **We'll rent** a car in Kiev.

2. The **type of transport** used to get somewhere = **на** + **prepositional case**. This type of sentence answers the question **Как/На чём?** (**See** the chapter "Prepositional Case," section II, B, in this grammar.) (p. 196)

3. To be **inside a closed vehicle** = **в** + **prepositional case**. (**See** the chapter "Prepositional Case," section II, C, in this grammar.) (p. 197)

4. To express **getting on** or **boarding** any type of transportation, **see** the chapter "Prefixed Verbs of Motion," section III, C, in this grammar (pp. 197, 250).

5. To express **getting off/out of** any type of transportation, **see** the chapter "Prefixed Verbs of Motion," section III, D, in this grammar (p. 250).

B. Movement by Vehicles (p. 249)

    1. Since vehicles move under their own power, they generally use the verb идти́/ходи́ть.

        a. Вот **идёт** авто́бус № 5. Here **comes**/There **goes** bus № 5.
        b. Э́тот по́езд **идёт** в Москву́. This train **is going** to Moscow.

    2. The main exception to this rule is **такси́**, which uses **е́хать/е́здить**.

        a. По у́лице **е́здят** мно́го такси́.
        Many taxis **are going up and down** the street.

        b. Э́то такси́ **е́дет** в Кремль. This taxi **is going** to the Kremlin.

C. **Translation of the Verb "to drive" in Russian** (p. 249)

    1. **е́хать/е́здить** are **intransitive** verbs and mean that the subject is going somewhere by vehicle, regardless of who is driving. For further clarification, use "на маши́не."

        a. Я ча́сто **е́зжу** на рабо́ту на маши́не. I frequently **drive** to work.
        b. За́втра Лари́са **е́дет** в Ки́ев. Larisa **is driving** to Kiev tomorrow.

    2. **везти́/вози́ть** are **transitive** verbs that mean the subject is driving **someone else** (the direct object [кого́]) somewhere.

             dir. obj.   dir. obj.
        a. Я **везу́** <u>её</u> в аэропо́рт. I **am taking/driving** <u>her</u> to the airport.

            dir. object   dir. object
        b. Мы **вози́ли** <u>дете́й</u> в цирк. We **drove/took** <u>the kids</u> to the circus.

    3. **вести́ маши́ну** refers to the phenomenon of driving a car at a certain point in time in one direction; **води́ть маши́ну** refers to knowing how to drive or to driving habitually. (The noun маши́ну can never be omitted from these phrases.)

        a. Кто **вёл маши́ну**, когда́ вы уви́дели ава́рию?
        Who **was driving** when you saw the accident?

        b. Ты уме́ешь **води́ть маши́ну**? Do you know how **to drive**?

D. To Travel Around/Throughout a Place = **путеше́ствовать + по + dative case** (где?) (p. 190)

Do not use в/на + accusative case with this verb to answer the question Куда́? To answer the question Куда́? use е́здить/е́хать/пое́хать + в/на + accusative case. The verb **е́здить** is synonymous with путеше́ствовать when followed by по + dative case of a noun denoting a state, country, or continent.

    1. Мы <u>путеше́ствовали</u> **по** Евро́пе. = Мы <u>е́здили</u> **по** Евро́пе.
    We <u>traveled</u> **around/throughout Europe.**

    2. **But:** В про́шлом году́ мы е́здили в Евро́пу. We went **to Europe** last year.

Глаго́лы движе́ния с приста́вками
Prefixed Verbs of Motion

I. Образова́ние и спряже́ние—Formation and Conjugation

The unprefixed verbs of motion that you learned in Chapter 8, such as идти́/ходи́ть and е́хать/е́здить, can be turned into prefixed verbs of motion by the addition of one of many verbal prefixes. It is important to remember that unlike unprefixed verbs of motion, which have two imperfective forms—one unidirectional (идти́), the other multidirectional (ходи́ть)—**prefixed verbs of motion have only ONE imperfective form** in addition to one perfective form. In this regard, they are like the great majority of Russian verbs. You are already familiar with some prefixed verbs of motion, such as приходи́ть (impf.)/прийти́ (pf.) and заходи́ть (impf.)/зайти́ (pf.).

    A. To form aspectual pairs, add a prefix to an unprefixed **multidirectional** verb of motion to create a prefixed **imperfective** verb of motion and add the same prefix to the unprefixed **unidirectional** verb of motion to get a prefixed **perfective** verb of motion (p. 225). Here is an example using the prefix **при-**, which means "arriving."

UNPREFIXED VERBS OF MOTION		PREFIXED VERBS OF MOTION		
Uni-directional Imperfective	Multi-directional Imperfective	Imperfective	Perfective	
идти́	ходи́ть	приходи́ть	прийти́[1]	to arrive by foot
е́хать	е́здить	приезжа́ть*	прие́хать	to arrive by vehicle
лете́ть	лета́ть	прилета́ть	прилете́ть	to arrive by plane/flying
плыть	пла́вать	приплыва́ть**	приплы́ть	to arrive by boat/swimming
бежа́ть	бе́гать	прибега́ть***	прибежа́ть	to arrive running
вести́	води́ть	приводи́ть	привести́	to bring/lead someone by foot
везти́	вози́ть	привози́ть	привезти́	to bring/transport by vehicle
нести́	носи́ть	приноси́ть	принести́	to bring/carry by foot

    B. Спряже́ние—Conjugation: Note the changes in the following unprefixed verbs of motion when they are used with prefixes (these changes apply to the verbs with asterisks after them in the list above). (p. 226)

    1. *е́здить

        a. When the unprefixed imperfective verb е́здить is used to form the imperfective of a prefixed verb of motion, it changes to -езжа́ть.

        b. For example, приезжа́ть conjugates

приезжа́ю	приезжа́ем
приезжа́ешь	приезжа́ете
приезжа́ет	приезжа́ют

---

[1] When the verb идти́ has a prefix added to it, it changes form to -йти́: идти́ → прийти́, зайти́, уйти́.

2. **пла́вать

a. When the unprefixed imperfective verb пла́вать is used to form the imperfective of a prefixed verb of motion, it changes to **-плыва́ть**.

b. For example, приплыва́ть conjugates

приплыва́ю	приплыва́ем
приплыва́ешь	приплыва́ете
приплыва́ет	приплыва́ют

3. ***бе́гать

a. When the unprefixed imperfective verb бе́гать is used to form the imperfective of a prefixed verb of motion, it has a stress change. The stress moves from the **e** to the **a**.

b. Note the difference in stress between the following two verbs:

бе́гаю	прибега́ю	бе́гаем	прибега́ем
бе́гаешь	прибега́ешь	бе́гаете	прибега́ете
бе́гает	прибега́ет	бе́гают	прибега́ют

II. Употребле́ние—Use

Remember that the concept of unidirectional vs. multidirectional motion does not apply to prefixed verbs of motion. Like almost all verbs in Russian, prefixed verbs of motion are subject to the rules of aspect usage you reviewed in chapters 3, 4, and 5. (**See** the chapter "Verbs: Aspect" in this grammar for a review of aspect usage.) Most prefixed verbs of motion belong to the group of verbs that express "reversible" actions; therefore, an imperfective verb in the past tense denotes a one-time action that has been reversed or annulled, and a perfective verb in the past tense denotes a one-time action that is still in effect. Thus, "Вчера́ к нам приезжа́ли го́сти" using an imperfective verb means that guests came to our place yesterday but are no longer there; "Вчера́ к нам прие́хали го́сти" using a perfective verb means that the guests are still visiting us (at this point in the narration of events). (**See** the chapter "Verbs: Aspect," sections I, A, 6, and I, B, 4, in this grammar for more information.) (pp. 226, 248)

In almost all cases, prefixed verbs of motion can be formed by adding a given prefix to any of the eight most common unprefixed verbs of motion. In order to conserve space, examples will be given using only one verb for each prefix. If you wish to see a given prefix used with several verbs of motion, consult the textbook, p. 227. In the examples below, the preposition (if any) and the case(s) that a particular verb governs are noted as well as the question word(s) associated with each verb.

A. Prefixed Verbs of Motion with **Paired** Directional Prefixes

1. The Prefixes **в**- (into) and **вы**- (out of) (p. 227)

a. входи́ть/войти́ (to go in, enter) + куда́? (в/на что)

куда́?
1'. Студе́нты <u>вошли́</u> в лаборато́рию.
The students <u>entered</u> **the laboratory**.

куда́?

2'. О́льга <u>вхо́дит</u> **на** по́чту. Olga <u>is going</u> **into the post office.**

b. **выходи́ть/вы́йти** (to exit, leave, go out) **+ отку́да? (из/с чего́)**
or **+ куда́? (в/на что)**

отку́да?

1'. Рабо́чие <u>выхо́дят</u> **с фа́брики** в три часа́.[2]
The workers <u>come out</u> **of the factory** at three.

куда́?

2'. Все <u>вы́шли</u> **во** двор (#). Everyone <u>went out</u> **to the courtyard.**

2. The Prefixes **при-** (arriving) and **у-** (departing, leaving) (p. 227)

a. **прилета́ть/прилете́ть** (to arrive flying) **+ куда́? (в/на что)/к кому́?**
or **+ отку́да? (из/с чего́)/от кого́?**

куда́?

1'. Она́ <u>прилете́ла</u> **в** Москву́ сего́дня у́тром.
She <u>arrived</u> **in Moscow** this morning.

отку́да?

2'. Самолёт <u>прилети́т</u> **с** Аля́ски в суббо́ту.
A plane <u>will arrive</u> **from Alaska** on Saturday.

b. **улета́ть/улете́ть** (to leave by plane/flying) **+ отку́да? (из/с чего́)**
or **куда́? (в/на что)**

отку́да?

1'. Мы <u>улета́ем</u> **из** Нью-Йо́рка в 4 часа́.
We <u>are departing</u> **(from) New York** at four o'clock.

отку́да?

2'. Вертолёт <u>улете́л</u> **со** стадио́на.
The helicopter <u>left</u> **(from) the stadium.**

куда́?

3'. Они́ <u>улета́ют</u> **в** Лос А́нжелес (#). They <u>are leaving</u> **for L.A.**

куда́?

4'. За́втра я <u>улечу́</u> **на** Аля́ску.
Tomorrow I <u>am leaving</u> **for Alaska.**

3. The Prefixes **под-** (approaching) and **от-** (movement away from) (pp. 236–37)

a. **подъезжа́ть/подъе́хать** (to approach by vehicle) **+ к кому́/чему́?**

к кому́?

1'. Маши́на <u>подъе́хала</u> **к** милиционе́ру.
The car <u>approached</u> **the police officer.**

---

[2] When mentioning the time of departure, use a verb with the prefix **вы-**.

к чему́?

2'. Мы <u>подъезжа́ем</u> **к** гаражу́. We <u>are driving up</u> **to the garage**.

b. **отбега́ть/отбежа́ть** (to run away from) + **от кого́/чего́?**

от чего́?

1'. Мы <u>отбежа́ли</u> **от** маши́ны. We <u>ran away</u> **from the car**.

от чего́?

2'. Я <u>отбежа́ла</u> **от** зда́ния. I <u>ran away</u> **from the building**.

c. With the transitive verbs **нести́, вести́,** and **везти́** the prefix **от-** adds the meaning of **taking someone or something from one place and leaving it in another.**

отвози́ть/отвезти́ (to take away, transport to another place) + **кого́/что? + куда́? (в/на что)**

кого́?   куда́?

1'. Я <u>отвёз</u> Ка́тю **в** аэропо́рт (#). I <u>took</u> **Katia to the airport**.

что?   куда́?

2'. Шофёр <u>отво́зит</u> кни́ги **на** по́чту.
The driver <u>is taking</u> **the books to the post office**.

4. The Prefixes **вз- (вс-, воз-, вос-)** (moving up) and **с-** (moving down from) (p. 244)

a. **взлета́ть/взлете́ть** (to fly up, take off)

1'. Самолёт уже́ <u>взлете́л</u>. The plane already <u>took off</u>.
2'. Ско́ро <u>взойдёт</u> со́лнце. Soon the sun <u>will rise</u>.

b. **сходи́ть/сойти́** (to come/walk down) + **отку́да? (с чего́)**

отку́да?

1'. Пассажи́ры <u>схо́дят</u> **с** самолёта.
The passengers <u>are getting off</u> **the plane**.

2'. идио́мы

a'. **сходи́ть/сойти́ с ума́** = to lose one's mind
Они́ сошли́ с ума́. They lost their minds.

b'. **своди́ть/свести́ кого́-то с ума́**
= to drive someone crazy

кого́?

Ты меня́ с ума́ сво́дишь. You are driving me crazy.

B. Prefixed Verbs of Motion with **Unpaired** Directional Prefixes

1. The Prefix **за-** + **к кому́?** or **куда́? (в/на что)** (dropping/stopping in); or + **за кем/чем?** (picking someone up/getting something) (p. 235)

к кому́?
a. Мы ча́сто <u>захо́дим</u> **к Ива́ну**. We frequently <u>drop in</u> **on Ivan**.

              куда́?   за чем?
b. Мы ча́сто <u>заезжа́ем</u> **в э́тот магази́н (#) за фру́ктами**.
We frequently <u>stop in</u> **at this store for fruit**.

за кем?
c. Я <u>зайду́</u> **за тобо́й** в 7 часо́в. I <u>will pick</u> **you** <u>up</u> at seven.

2. The Prefix **пере-** + **что?** or **че́рез что?** (movement across);
or **переходи́ть/перейти́** + **на но́вую рабо́ту** = to change jobs;
or **переезжа́ть/перее́хать** + **куда́?** (**в/на что** or **на но́вую кварти́ру/
в но́вый дом**) = to move (p. 235)

(че́рез) что?
a. Ученики́ <u>перехо́дят</u> (**че́рез**) **у́лицу**.
The students <u>are crossing</u> **the street**.

куда́?
b. Моя́ сестра́ <u>перешла́</u> **на но́вую рабо́ту**.
My sister <u>has taken</u> **a new job**.

куда́?
c. Моя́ семья́ <u>переезжа́ет</u> **в Бо́стон (#)**.
My family <u>is moving</u> **to Boston**.

3. The Prefix **про-** + **куда́?** (**в/на что** or **к чему́**) (to get somewhere);[3]
or + **что?** (passing something unintentionally);
or + **ми́мо чего́?** (going past);
or + **че́рез что?** (passing through);
or + **по чему́?** (moving along something) (p. 228)

          куда́?   куда́?
a. Как <u>пройти́</u> **на Кра́сную пло́щадь (#)**?[3] Как <u>пройти́</u> **к музе́ю**?[3]
How <u>do</u> you <u>get</u> **to Red Square**? How <u>do</u> you <u>get</u> **to the museum**?

что?
b. Лари́са <u>прое́хала</u> **свою́ остано́вку**. Larisa <u>missed</u> **her stop**.

ми́мо чего́?
c. Тури́сты <u>проходи́ли</u> **ми́мо музе́я**.
The tourists <u>were walking</u> **past the museum**.

че́рез что?
d. Вчера́ я <u>прошла́</u> **че́рез парк (#)**.
Yesterday I <u>walked</u> **through the park**.

---

[3] Use **в/на что** when the destination is an open space and **к чему́** when the destination is a building or group of buildings.

по чему́?

e. Его́ грузови́к <u>прое́дет</u> **по** на́шей у́лице.
His truck <u>will pass</u> **along our street**.

4. The Prefix до- + **до чего́?** (moving as far as, reaching a goal) (p. 228)

до чего́?

a. Тури́сты <u>дошли́</u> **до** Кра́сной пло́щади.
The tourists <u>walked</u> **up to (as far as)** **Red Square**.

до чего́?

b. <u>Доезжа́й</u> **до** сле́дующей у́лицы. <u>Drive</u> **up to the next street**.

до чего́?

c. Че́рез 20 мину́т мы <u>дойдём</u> **до** стадио́на.
We'<u>ll get</u> **to the stadium** in 20 minutes.

C. The Prefix **с-** in the Meaning of a "Quick Round Trip"

1. The prefix **с-** **combines with unprefixed multidirectional verbs of motion to form perfective verbs that indicate quick motion somewhere and back** (a, below). Also use **с-**prefixed **perfective** verbs of motion in the past tense when referring to previously mentioned or contemplated actions or the result of an action; otherwise use multidirectional imperfectives like **ходи́ть** (b, below). (pp. 245, 246)

    a. **сходи́ть**

        1'. Она́ сходи́ла домо́й за деньга́ми.
        She **ran home** for her money (**and is now back**).

        2'. Он **схо́дит** в магази́н и пото́м бу́дет гото́вить обе́д.
        He **will run** to the store and then (**come back and**) make supper.

    b. **сходи́ть** vs. **ходи́ть**

        1'. Вы наконе́ц **сходи́ли** в библиоте́ку за кни́гой?
        Did you finally **run down** to the library for that book?

        2'. **But:**

            a'. Что вы **де́лали** вчера́ ве́чером?
            What **did** you **do** last night?

            b'. Мы **ходи́ли** на ле́кцию.
            We **went** to a lecture.

2. **Note:** When you include perfectives formed with the prefix **с-**, **unprefixed verbs of motion have five forms**, two imperfective and three perfective. Using the verb "to go by foot" as an example, they are

    a. **идти́** unidirectional imperfective (motion in one direction)

        Он **идёт** в библиоте́ку. He **is going** to the library.

b. **ходи́ть** multidirectional imperfective (round-trip motion, general motion)

> Она́ ча́сто **хо́дит** в библиоте́ку.
> She frequently **goes** to the library.

c. **пойти́** perfective formed from unidirectional imperfective (setting off/starting out or completion of one-way trip)

> Они́ **пошли́** в библиоте́ку.
> They **set off** for/**went** to the library.

d. **походи́ть** perfective from multidirectional imperfective (to engage in general motion "for a while")

> Они́ вста́ли и **походи́ли**.
> They got up and **walked around a bit**.

e. **сходи́ть** perfective from multidirectional imperfective (to go somewhere and back quickly or used when referring to previously mentioned or contemplated actions or the result of an action)

> Она́ **сходи́ла** в библиоте́ку и пото́м начала́ занима́ться.
> She **went** to the library and then **(came back and)** began to study.

III. Modes of Transportation

A. Expressing **How** or **By What Means** of Transportation you are Traveling (p. 196)

To answer the question **На чём?/Как?** use the preposition **на** + **prepositional case**. (**See** the chapter "Prepositional Case," section II, B, in this grammar.)

B. Expressing **Being in a Closed Vehicle** (p. 197)

To answer the question **Где?** (**Where/In what kind of vehicle** are/were you?), use the preposition **в** + **prepositional case**. (**See** the chapter "Prepositional Case," section II, C, in this grammar.)

C. Expressing **Getting on** or **Boarding** any Type of Transportation

1. Use the verb **сади́ться/сесть**. Оле́г **сади́тся** (Oleg **is getting on/in**) . . . (p. 197)

a. With **такси́** and **маши́на** use **в** + **accusative case**.

1'. . . . в такси́.
2'. . . . в маши́ну.

b. With **авто́бус, по́езд, метро́**, and **самолёт** use either **в** or **на** + **accusative case**.

1'. . . . **в/на** авто́бус (#).
2'. . . . **в/на** метро́.

3'. ... **в/на** самолёт (#).
4'. ... **в/на** по́езд (#).

c. With **велосипе́д, мотоци́кл, мотороллер** (scooter), **парохо́д, кора́бль,** and **ло́шадь** use **на** + **accusative case.**

1'. ... **на** велосипе́д (#).
2'. ... **на** мотоци́кл (#) или **на** мотороллер (#).
3'. ... **на** парохо́д (#) или **на** кора́бль (#).
4'. ... **на** ло́шадь (#).

2. In addition to **сади́ться/сесть,** you may also use the verb **входи́ть/войти́** + **в** + **accusative case** to express getting on/in any **closed** vehicle (p. 250).

a. Я вошёл **в** авто́бус (#). I got **on the bus**.
b. Я вошла́ **в** трамва́й (#). I got **on the streetcar**.

D. Expressing **Getting Off** or **Out of** any Type of Transportation (p. 250)

1. With **авто́бус, тролле́йбус, трамва́й, по́езд, маши́на,** and **такси́** use the verb **выходи́ть/вы́йти** + **из** + **genitive case.**

a. Тури́сты вы́шли **из** по́езда.
The tourists got **out of/off the train**.

b. А́нна уви́дела своего́ дру́га, когда́ он выходи́л **из** маши́ны.
Anna caught sight of her friend as he was getting **out of a car**.

2. With **кора́бль** and **парохо́д** use the verb **сходи́ть/сойти́** + **с** + **genitive case**. You may also use this construction with **самолёт**.

a. Когда́ мы пришли́, пассажи́ры уже́ сходи́ли **с** парохо́да.
When we arrived, passengers were already getting **off the ship**.

b. Я сошёл **с** корабля́ в Нью-Йо́рке.
I got **off the ship** in New York.

3. With **велосипе́д, мотоци́кл, мотороллер,** and **ло́шадь** use the verb **слеза́ть/слезть** + **genitive case.**

a. Де́вочка сле́зла **с** велосипе́да. The girl got **off her bike**.

b. Мои́ бра́тья всегда́ слеза́ют **с** мотороллеров на том перекрёстке.
My brothers always get **off their scooters** at that intersection.

Прича́стия—Participles (Verbal Adjectives)

I. Оконча́ния/образова́ние—Endings/Formation

There are four types of participles in Russian (p. 168).

A. Прича́стия настоя́щего вре́мени действи́тельного зало́га—Present Active Participles are only formed from **imperfective verbs** (p. 170).

1. Remove the -**т** from the third-person plural (они́) form of the verb.		2. Add -**щ**- plus the proper adjective ending
чита́ю(т)	→	чита́ющий
говоря́(т)	→	говоря́щая
живу́(т)	→	живу́щее
пи́шу(т)	→	пи́шущие

B. Прича́стия проше́дшего вре́мени действи́тельного зало́га—Past Active Participles are formed from both **imperfective** and **perfective** verbs (pp. 170–71).

1. Remove the -**л** from the masculine past-tense form.		2. Add -**вш**- plus the proper adjective ending.	**OR**, if the masculine past tense does not end in an -**л**, add just -**ш**- + adj. endings.
чита́(л)	→	чита́вший	
говори́(л)	→	говори́вшая	
сказа́(л)	→	сказа́вшие	
писа́(л)	→	писа́вший	
написа́(л)	→	написа́вшее	
помо́г	→	помо́гший	
принёс	→	принёсшая	
привы́к	→	привы́кшие	

Note the past active participles formed from the verb **идти́** and its prefixed forms.

идти́	→	**ше́дший**
пройти́	→	**проше́дшая**
найти́	→	**наше́дшие**

C. Прича́стия настоя́щего вре́мени страда́тельного зало́га—Present Passive Participles are formed only from **imperfective transitive** verbs (p. 174).[1]

1. Use the first-person plural (мы) form of the verb.		2. Add the proper adjective ending.
лю́бим	→	люби́мый = favorite
(так) называ́ем	→	(так) называ́емое = (so-) called
уважа́ем	→	уважа́емые = dear, respected

---

[1] Present passive participles are used mainly in "formal" written Russian although some are frequently used as adjectives. Some of the most often-used forms of this participle, including those noted above, are незабыва́емый (unforgettable), незави́симый (independent), and необходи́мый (necessary, essential).

D. Причáстия прошéдшего врéмени страдáтельного залóга—Past Passive Participles are only formed from **transitive perfective** verbs. **There are three types of endings.** (p. 175)

1. **Type 1: -т-** is the ending for **first-conjugation verbs with infinitives ending in -ить** or **-ыть** and **first-conjugation verbs** that contain an **-н-** or an **-м- infix**. (For example, начáть: начнý, начнёшь, начнýт or понять: поймý, поймёшь, поймýт.)

a. Remove the soft sign from the infinitive.		b. Add the proper adjective ending.
откры́т(ь)	→	откры́тый
забы́т(ь)	→	забы́тая
уби́т(ь)	→	уби́тые
начáт(ь)	→	нáчатые
нали́т(ь)	→	нáлитая
одéт(ь)	→	одéтый

2. **Type 2: -нн-** is the ending for **first-conjugation verbs with infinitives ending in -ать/-ять** (other than those with an -н- or an -м- infix [type 1 verbs, above]) and for **second-conjugation verbs with infinitives ending in -еть**.

a. Remove the -ть from the infinitive.		b. Add -нн- plus the proper adjective ending.
сдéла(ть)	→	сдéланный
прочитá(ть)	→	прочи́танная
написá(ть)	→	напи́санные
да(ть)	→	дáнное
потеря́(ть)	→	потéрянный
уви́де(ть)	→	уви́денный

Note on stress: If the infinitive ending (-ать/-ять or -еть) is stressed, the stress moves one syllable back (to the left) in the past passive participle. For example, прочитáть → прочи́танный.

3. **Type 3: -енн-** (unstressed)/**-ённ-** (stressed) are the endings for **second-conjugation verbs with infinitives ending in -ить** and for **first-conjugation verbs with infinitives ending in -сти́ (-сть)** or **-зти́**.

a. Remove the ending from the first-person singular (я) form of the verb.			b. Add -енн- (or -ённ- if the ending is stressed) plus adjective ending.
реши́ть	реш(ý)	→	решённый
купи́ть	купл(ю́)	→	кýпленная
встрéтить	встрéч(у)	→	встрéченное
принести́	принес(ý)	→	принесённая
привезти́	привез(ý)	→	привезённые
украсть	украд(ý)	→	украденный

Note on stress: Second-conjugation verbs with shifting stress (купи́ть: куплю́, кýпишь, кýпят) take the stress of the **second-person singular** in the past passive participle (кýпленный). First-conjugation verbs ending in **-сть** have the stress of the feminine past tense: укрáла → укрáденный.

E. **Short-Form Past Passive Participles** (p. 176)

The past passive participle has a short form that resembles the short-form adjective in form and function. **The short form of the past passive participle uses short-form adjective endings (masculine -#, feminine -a, neuter -o, plural -ы) and may only be used as a predicate**, that is in the structure: subject (in nominative case) + a form of the verb быть (which isn't expressed in Russian in the present tense) + short-form past passive participle. (In English translation this would read subject + linking verb [usually a form of the verb "to be" or "to have"] + participle.)[2]

1. Дверь **закры́та**. The door **is closed**.
2. Э́тот дом **кýплен**. This house **has been bought**.
3. Де́ньги **полýчены**. The money **has been received**.

Note: Short-form past passive participles use only one -**н**- where a corresponding long-form past passive participle would use two -**нн**-.

II. Употребле́ние—Use

A. General Characteristics of Participles

1. Participles are sometimes called "verbal adjectives," which is an apt way of describing them. All participles in Russian are **derived from verbs** and have the **endings of adjectives**.

2. **Participles are used to modify nouns** and therefore **agree** with the noun they modify in **gender, case,** and **number**: в закры́том магази́не (in the closed store), на закры́той две́ри (on the closed door), у закры́того окна́ (by the closed window). (p. 171)

3. Both **active** participles (present and past) qualify a noun that is the performer (agent) of the action denoted in the participle (p. 168): "**Спя́щая** краса́вица"— "**Sleeping** Beauty" (the Beauty is the one who is sleeping).

4. Both **passive** participles (present and past) modify a noun that is the recipient of the action denoted in the participle (p. 168): **закры́тая** дверь—the **closed** door (the door hasn't closed itself but rather has been closed by someone/something else).

5. **All long-form participles may modify a noun that is of any gender, case, or number**. The following examples contain present active participles, but the same idea also holds true for the other three types of participles. (p. 169)

        nom. pl.   nom. pl.
a. Вот студе́нты, <u>живу́щие</u> в на́шем общежи́тии.
Here are the students (<u>who are</u>) <u>living</u> in our dormitory.

        fem. acc. sg. fem. acc. sg.
b. Я ви́жу студе́нтку, <u>живу́щую</u> в на́шем общежи́тии.
I see the student (<u>who is</u>) <u>living</u> in our dormitory.

---

[2] See the chapter "Sentence Structure," section, I, B, in this grammar for a review of predicates in Russian.

      masc. gen. sg. masc. gen. sg.

c. Э́то для студе́нт**а**, <u>живу́щ**его**</u> в на́шем общежи́тии.
This is for the student (<u>who is</u>) <u>living</u> in our dormitory.

      prep. pl. prep. pl.

d. Я говорю́ о студе́нт**ах**, <u>живу́щ**их**</u> в на́шем общежи́тии.
I am talking about the students (<u>who are</u>) <u>living</u> in our dormitory.

      fem. dat. sg. fem. dat. sg.

e. Я дам э́ту кни́гу студе́нтк**е**, <u>живу́щ**ей**</u> в на́шем общежи́тии.
I will give this book to the student (<u>who is</u>) <u>living</u> in our dormitory.

      masc. instr. sg. masc. instr. sg.

f. Мы дово́льны студе́нт**ом**, <u>живу́щ**им**</u> в на́шем общежи́тии.
We are satisfied with the student (<u>who is</u>) <u>living</u> in our dormitory.

B. Specifics

1. As the examples in section II, A, 2–5, show, participles may be used either **before** the noun they modify or **after** it (p. 171). When a participle comes before the noun it modifies, it is generally translated without the aid of a relative pronoun: **закры́тая** дверь—the **closed** door. It is more common, however, to see participles **after** the noun they modify. In such cases, they are often translated with the use of "who," "which," or "that." (**See** the examples in II, A, 5, above.)

2. Replacing Participles with **кото́рый** Clauses

  a. An **active** participle in any case can be replaced by the **nominative** form of the relative pronoun **кото́рый** and a finite form of the **verb** (past or present tense) from which the participle is derived (p. 172).

   1'. Вот студе́нты, **живу́щие** (nom.) в на́шем общежи́тии.

   2'. Я ви́жу студе́нтов, **живу́щих** (acc.) в на́шем общежи́тии.

   3'. Э́то для студе́нтов, **живу́щих** (gen.) в на́шем общежи́тии.

   4'. Я говорю́ о студе́нтах, **живу́щих** (prep.) в на́шем общежи́тии.

   5'. Мы да́ли кни́гу студе́нтам, **живу́щим** (dat.) в на́шем общежи́тии.

   6'. Мы дово́льны студе́нтами, **живу́щими** (instr.) в на́шем общежи́тии.

   Note: Each of the participles in the six sentences above can be replaced by the phrase **кото́рые** (nom.) **живу́т**: Я говорю́ о студе́нтах, **кото́рые живу́т** в на́шем общежи́тии.

  b. A long-form **passive** participle can be replaced by an **accusative** form of the relative pronoun **кото́рый** and a finite form of the **verb** (in the proper tense) from which the participle is derived.

1'. Вот кни́га, **напи́санная** (nom.) **им.**
2'. Я ви́жу кни́гу, **напи́санную** (acc.) **им.**
3'. У меня́ нет кни́ги, **напи́санной** (gen.) **им.**
4'. Я говорю́ о кни́ге, **напи́санной** (prep.) **им.**
5'. Я пишу́ рабо́те по кни́ге, **напи́санной** (dat.) **им.**
6'. Я ду́маю над кни́гой, **напи́санной** (instr.) **им.**

Note: The bold portions in each of the above sentences can be replaced by **кото́рую** (acc.) **он написа́л:** Вот кни́га, **кото́рую он написа́л.**

Note: With passive participles, the agent of the action (in this case, "he" [**им**]) is in instrumental case (p. 175). When the passive participle is replaced by кото́рый + verb, the resulting clause is in active voice with the agent therefore in nominative case (**он**).

Дееприча́стия—Verbal Adverbs

I. Оконча́ния/образова́ние—Endings/Formation (p. 178)

There are two types of verbal adverbs in Russian. Both are fixed (non-changing) forms. They do not have tense, but they do express aspect.

A. Дееприча́стия несоверше́нного ви́да—Imperfective (Simultaneous) Verbal Adverbs are only formed from **imperfective** verbs. They denote action that occurs **simultaneously** with the action of the verb in the main clause of the sentence.

1. Remove the ending of the third-person plural (они́) form of the verb.		2. Add **-я** (**-а** after "hushers" [ж, ч, ш, щ]).	3. If the verb is reflexive, add **-сь**.
чита́(ют)	→	чита́я	
жив(у́т)	→	живя́	
пока́зыва(ют)	→	пока́зывая	
говор(я́т)	→	говоря́	
спеш(а́т)	→	спеша́	
занима́(ют)ся	→		занима́ясь

Note: -авать-type verbs retain the -ва- suffix in the imperfective verbal adverb.

встава́ть	(встаю́т)	→	встава́я
дава́ть	(даю́т)	→	дава́я
узнава́ть	(узнаю́т)	→	узнава́я

B. Дееприча́стия соверше́нного ви́да—Perfective (Sequential) Verbal Adverbs are only formed from **perfective** verbs. They denote action that is completed **before** the action expressed in the main clause of the sentence.

1. Remove the -л from the masculine past tense.		2. Add **-в**	**OR**, if the verb is reflexive, remove -лся and add -**вшись**.	**OR**, if the masculine past tense does not end in an -л, add -**ши**.
прочита́(л)	→	прочита́в		
написа́(л)	→	написа́в		
посмотре́(л)	→	посмотре́в		
пригото́ви(л)	→	пригото́вив		
верну́(лся)		→	верну́вшись	
улыбну́(лся)		→	улыбну́вшись	
помо́г		→		помо́гши
принёс		→		принёсши
привы́к		→		привы́кши

Note: Prefixed forms of **идти** form perfective verbal adverbs from the stem of the third-person plural (они) form of the verb with the ending **-я**.

Infinitive	Third-Person Plural		Perfective Verbal Adverb
зайти́	зайд(у́т)	→	зайдя́
найти́	найд(у́т)	→	найдя́
прийти́	прид(у́т)	→	придя́
уйти́	уйд(у́т)	→	уйдя́

II. Употреблéние—Use

For both imperfective and perfective verbal adverbs, the action they express is performed by the subject of the main verb (the verb in the main clause).

A. Imperfective (Simultaneous) verbal adverbs . . .

1. are formed only from **imperfective** verbs and denote an action that occurs **simultaneously** with the action of the verb in the main clause of the sentence (p. 176).

2. Frequently, imperfective verbal adverbs are translated using the English word "while."

a. **Слу́шая** му́зыку, я чита́ла газéту.
While listening to music, I read the newspaper.

b. **Говоря́** с Ивáном, я смотрéла ему́ в глазá.
While talking with Ivan, I looked him square in the face.

B. Perfective (Sequential) verbal adverbs . . .

1. are formed only from **perfective** verbs and denote an action that has been completed **prior to** the action expressed in the main clause of the sentence (p. 176).

2. Quite often, perfective verbal adverbs are translated with the aid of the English word "having"; however, note the numerous possible translations of the same perfective verbal adverb (p. 179).

Дав мне письмó, он ушёл.

a. **Having given** me the letter, he left.
b. **On giving** me the letter, he left.
c. **After giving** me the letter, he left.
d. **When he had given** me the letter, he left.
e. **He gave** me the letter and left.

Имена́ прилага́тельные—Adjectives

Russian adjectives, like adjectives in English, have three **degrees**.

1) The **positive** degree expresses a given quality: Э́то **но́вый** дом. = This is a **new** house.

2) The **comparative** degree compares two things: Э́тот дом нове́е/бо́лее но́вый, чем наш. = This house is **newer** than ours.

3) The **superlative** expresses the highest degree of a given quality: Э́то **са́мый но́вый** дом на у́лице. = This is the **newest** house on the street.

I. Положи́тельная сте́пень—The Positive Degree

A. По́лные фо́рмы—Long Forms

1. The long forms of Russian adjectives agree with the noun they modify in gender, case, and number. **See** the chapter "Adjectives: Sample Declensions" in this grammar for a complete listing of long-form adjective declensions. (p. 263)

2. Long forms may be used either to modify a noun **attributively** or to modify a noun or pronoun as a **predicate adjective**.

   a. **Attributively**: The adjective usually comes immediately before the noun.

      1'. Я ви́жу **но́вую** кни́гу. I see the **new** book.
      2'. Они́ живу́т в **ста́ром** до́ме. They live in an **old** house.

   b. **As a Predicate**: subject + linking verb [usually a form of быть] + predicate adjective) (**See** the chapter "Sentence Structure," section I, B, in this grammar for an explanation of what constitutes a predicate.)

      1'. Твоя́ кни́га **но́вая**. Your book is **new**.
      2'. Э́тот дом **ма́ленький**. This house is **small**.

3. **Compound adjectives** can be formed in the following ways:

   a. To link two adjectives, add an -o ending to the stem of the first adjective and join it to the second adjective with a hyphen (pp. 102, 127).

      1'. **ру́сско-англи́йский** слова́рь = a Russian-English dictionary
      2'. **чёрно-бе́лый** телеви́зор = a black-and-white television
      3'. **све́тло-зелёное** кре́сло = a light green chair
      4'. **тёмно-си́ний** костю́м = a dark blue (navy blue) suit

   b. To use the numeral "one" to form a compound adjective, add the neuter nominative form of the numeral (одно́) to the adjective (p. 112).

      1'. **одномото́рный** самолёт = a **single**-engine aircraft
      2'. **одноа́ктная** пье́са = a **one**-act play

c. To use a cardinal numeral other than "one"—such as two, three, four, five, etc.—to form a compound adjective, add the **genitive** form of the number (двух, трёх, четырёх, пяти́) to the adjective (p. 112).[1]

    1'. двухэта́жный дом = a **two**-story house
    2'. трёхко́мнатная кварти́ра = a **three**-room apartment
    3'. пятиле́тний план = a **five**-year plan

B. Кра́ткие фо́рмы—Short Forms

1. Forms

a. Short-form adjectives agree with their subject in gender and number. They are only used as **predicates** (p. 263).[2]

b. The endings for short-form adjectives are fixed forms. They are

1'. masculine	-#:	нов	мил	гото́в
2'. neuter	-о:	но́во	ми́ло	гото́во
3'. feminine	-а:	нова́	мила́	гото́ва
4'. plural	-ы:	но́вы	ми́лы	гото́вы

c. The adjectives **большо́й** and **ма́ленький** have special short forms.

    1'. большо́й: вели́к   велика́   велико́   велики́
    2'. ма́ленький: мал   мала́   мало́   малы́

2. **Remember** these commonly used short-form adjectives (pp. 263–64):

a. благода́рен, благода́рна/ы кому́   grateful **to someone**
Мы **им** так благода́рны.[3]

b. бо́лен, больна́, больны́ **чем**   ill/sick **with something**
Она́ больна́ гри́ппом.

c. го́лоден, голодна́, го́лодны   hungry

d. гото́в, гото́ва, гото́вы **к чему́**   to be prepared/ready **for something**
Он гото́в к экза́мену.

e. дово́лен, дово́льна, дово́льны **кем/чем**   satisfied **with someone/ something**
Они́ дово́льны студе́нтами.

f. до́лжен, должна́, должны́ + **infinitive**   must, ought to
Мы должны́ им **помо́чь**.

---

[1] For a review of the genitive case of cardinal numerals, **see** the chapter "Review: The Declension of Numerals," sections I–VI, in this grammar.

[2] **See** the chapter "Sentence Structure," section I, B, in this grammar for an explanation of what constitutes a predicate.

[3] **Remember** that так and как are used with short-form adjectives.

g. жена́т, жена́ты **на ком** (masculine and plural only)	to be married **to someone** И́горь жена́т **на О́льге.**
h. жив, жива́, жи́вы	alive
i. за́нят, занята́, за́няты	busy, occupied
j. здоро́в, здоро́ва, здоро́вы	healthy, well
k. ну́жен, нужна́, ну́жно, нужны́ **что** <u>кому́</u>	need <u>Мне</u> нужны́ э́ти кни́ги.
l. похо́ж, похо́жа, похо́жи **на кого́**	to be like/similar **to someone** Она́ похо́жа **на отца́.**
m. прав, права́, пра́вы не прав, не права́, не пра́вы	correct, right incorrect, wrong
n. ра́д/а/ы + **infinitive** or **кому́/чему́** (short form only)	happy, glad Я рад вас **ви́деть.** Я **вам** рад.
o. свобо́ден, свобо́дна, свобо́дны	free, not occupied
p. серди́т/а/ы **на кого́**	angry **with someone** Он серди́т **на Ле́ну.**
q. согла́сен, согла́сна/ы **с кем/чем** (short form only)	agree **with someone/-thing** Они́ **со мной** согла́сны.
r. сча́стлив, сча́стлива, сча́стливы	happy
s. сыт, сыта́, сы́ты	full (not hungry)
t. уве́рен, уве́рена, уве́рены	sure, certain

3. Use

a. **Short-form adjectives are only used as predicate adjectives.** In other words, they are only used in the construction **subject + linking verb** (usually a form of быть) **+ short-form adjective** (pp. 263–64). (**See** the chapter "Sentence Structure," section I, B, in this grammar for an explanation of what constitutes a predicate.) **Remember** that the present tense of быть is not expressed in Russian.

1'. Он (#) был бо́лен (#). He was **sick.**
2'. Она́ права́. She is **right.**
3'. Они́ сча́стливы. They are **happy.**

b. **Remember** that short-form adjectives modifying всё or э́то will be neuter; those modifying кто will be masculine.

1'. Э́то/Всё интере́сно. This/Everything is **interesting.**
2'. Кто гото́в (#)? Who is **ready?**

c. In addition, when the following short-form adjectives refer to clothing, they have the additional meaning of "too big" or "too small."

too big	too small	too wide	too narrow	too long	too short
вели́к	мал	широ́к	у́зок	дли́нен	ко́роток
велика́	мала́	широка́	узка́	длинна́	коротка́
велико́	мало́	широко́	узко́	длинно́	ко́ротко
велики́	малы́	широки́	узки́	длинны́	коротки́

1'. Пальто́ **велико́/мало́**. The overcoat is **too big/too small**.

2'. Э́ти брю́ки **длинны́/коротки́**.
These pants are **too long/too small** (**short**).

II. Сравни́тельная сте́пень—The Comparative Degree

In English, there are primarily two ways to create the comparative forms of adjectives. 1) The **simple comparative** is a one-word form that adds the suffix -**er** to the positive degree of the adjective: new → new**er**. 2) The **compound comparative** is a two-word form that uses the comparative words "**more**" or "**less**" plus the positive form of the adjective: interesting → **more/less** interesting. **Note** that adjectives in English form comparatives using one of these models or the other, not both. For example, we do not say "more new" or "interestinger."

In Russian, adjectives (and adverbs) also form simple and compound comparatives, but the difference is that **most adjectives can form both types of comparative** (p. 268). The **simple** comparative replaces the ending of the positive form of the adjective with a comparative ending: но́вый → нове́е, дорого́й → доро́же, whereas the **compound** comparative uses the comparative words **бо́лее/ме́нее** (more/less) plus the positive form of the adjective: но́вый → **бо́лее** но́вый.

A. The Compound Comparative (p. 268)

1. Formation: Place the **indeclinable** word **бо́лее** (more) or **ме́нее**[4] (less) before the positive degree of the adjective.

2. Use: Compound comparatives can be used in any gender, case, and number either attributively or as a predicate. The words **бо́лее** and **ме́нее** do not decline, but the positive form of the adjective declines to agree with the noun it modifies.

a. Это **бо́лее** но́вый дом (#). This is a **newer** house.

b. У них **ме́нее** интере́сная жизнь (#), чем у нас.
Their life is **less interesting** than ours.

c. Я ви́жу **бо́лее** ста́рую маши́ну в гараже́.
I see the **older** car in the garage.

d. Они́ говоря́т о **бо́лее** лёгком зада́нии.
They are talking about the **easier** assignment.

---

[4] **Remember** that there is only one way in Russian to say "less" + adjective or adverb: you must use the compound comparative form with **ме́нее**. Э́та информа́ция **ме́нее ва́жная**, чем та информа́ция.

B. The Simple Comparative

1. Formation: Simple comparatives are formed in one of two ways.

a. **-e** ending (p. 270)

1'. If the final consonant of the adjective stem is **к, г, х, т,** or **д,** the ending of the simple comparative is **-e** and the final consonant(s) of the stem will undergo an alternation: **к, т → ч; г, з, д → ж; с, х → ш; ст → щ.** (These are the same consonant alternations you learned for the conjugation of verbs.)

Note: If the final letters of the adjective stem are **-к** or **-ок,** they sometimes drop and the preceding consonant undergoes an alternation. It is not possible to determine which adjectives drop the **-к** or **-ок** by looking at the positive form of the adjective.

a'. **к, т → ч**

Positive Form		Comparative
1". бога́тый (rich)	→	бога́че
2". гро́мкий (loud)	→	гро́мче
3". жа́ркий (hot)	→	жа́рче
4". коро́ткий (short)	→	коро́че (-к- drops)
5". лёгкий (easy)	→	ле́гче

b'. **г, з, д → ж**

Positive Form		Comparative
1". бли́зкий (close)	→	бли́же (-к- drops)
2". дорого́й (expensive)	→	доро́же
3". молодо́й (young)	→	моло́же
4". ни́зкий (low)	→	ни́же (-к- drops)
5". твёрдый (hard)	→	тве́рже
6". у́зкий (narrow)	→	у́же (-к- drops)

c'. **с, х → ш**

Positive Form		Comparative
1". высо́кий (tall)	→	вы́ше (-ок- drops)
2". ти́хий (quiet)	→	ти́ше

d'. **ст → щ**

Positive Form		Comparative
1". просто́й (simple)	→	про́ще
2". ча́стый (frequent)	→	ча́ще

2'. Some comparative forms have unpredictable stem changes and must be memorized.

Positive Form		Comparative
a'. далёкий (far, distant) →		да́льше
b'. дешёвый (cheap)	→	деше́вле

	Positive Form			Comparative
c'.	молодо́й	(young)	→	мла́дше
d'.	по́здний	(late)	→	по́зже, поздне́е
e'.	ра́нний	(early)	→	ра́ньше
f'.	ста́рый	(old)	→	ста́рше

b. **-ee (-ей)** ending: If the final consonant of an adjective stem is **anything other than** к, г, х, т, or д, the simple comparative ending is **-ee**, and the final consonant of the stem will **not** undergo a change (p. 268).

	Positive Form		Comparative		Positive Form		Comparative
1'.	сла́бый	→	слабе́е	4'.	у́мный	→	умне́е
2'.	све́жий	→	свеже́е	5'.	глу́пый	→	глупе́е
3'.	ми́лый	→	миле́е	6'.	бы́стрый	→	быстре́е

Note: As you can see from the above examples, the stress for this type of the simple comparative generally moves to the ending: **-ée**. You should memorize the following adjectives in which the stress **does not** move to the ending: краси́вее, интере́снее, ме́дленнее, прия́тнее, серьёзнее, удо́бнее, ужа́снее.

c. **Exceptional Forms:** Four common adjectives have exceptional simple comparative forms (p. 269).

	Positive Form	Adverb	Comparative
1'.	большо́й	мно́го	бо́льше
2'.	ма́ленький	ма́ло	ме́ньше
3'.	хоро́ший	хорошо́	лу́чше
4'.	плохо́й	пло́хо	ху́же

Note: Use **бо́льше**, not **лу́чше**, in comparisons with the verbs **люби́ть** and **нра́виться**.

Я люблю́ литерату́ру **бо́льше**, чем нау́ку.
I like literature **more** (**better**) than science.

Мне понра́вилась пье́са **бо́льше**, чем конце́рт.
I liked the play **more** (**better**) than the concert.

2. **Use:** Since the simple form of the comparative does not decline, **it can only be used as a predicate** (p. 268). That is, it can only be used in the structure: subject of the sentence + a linking verb [usually a form of быть] + short form comparative. **Remember** that the present tense of быть is not expressed in Russian.

a. Э́тот велосипе́д **нове́е**, чем мой.
This bike is **newer** than mine.

b. Чика́го **бли́же**, чем Нью-Йо́рк.
Chicago is **closer** than New York.

c. Мой оте́ц был **вы́ше**, чем я.
My father was **taller** than I am.

Note: Using **мла́дше** vs. **моло́же** and **ста́рше** vs. **бо́лее ста́рый** (p. 271)

Use **мла́дше** when comparing siblings; otherwise use **моло́же**.

> Мой брат **мла́дше** меня́.
> My brother is **younger** than I am.

> Га́ля **моло́же**, чем Серёжа.
> Galia is younger than Seriozha.

Use **ста́рше** when comparing animate nouns and **бо́лее ста́рый** when comparing things.

> Серёжа **ста́рше**, чем Га́ля.
> Seriozha is **older** than Galia.

> Э́та кни́га **бо́лее ста́рая**, чем та кни́га.
> This book is **older** than that one.

Note: The adjectives **хоро́ший, плохо́й, молодо́й,** and **ста́рый** have special adjectival comparative forms that can modify nouns in any gender, case, and number (p. 271).

> хоро́ший → **лу́чший**; плохо́й → **ху́дший**

> У них **лу́чшее/ху́дшее** реше́ние, чем у нас.
> They have a **better/worse** solution than we do.

> молодо́й → **мла́дший**; ста́рый → **ста́рший**

> У Ва́ни одна́ **мла́дшая/ста́ршая** сестра́.
> Vania has one **younger/older** sister.

C. How to Express **Comparisons** in Russian

1. **"than"**: There are two ways to express the concept "than" in Russian (p. 269).

   a. Expressing the Second Half of the Comparison by using **Genitive Case**

   Note: You may only use this construction when 1) both parts of the comparison are nouns or pronouns and 2) the first part of the comparison is in nominative case.

   >   nom.   gen.
   > 1'. Наш дом нове́е ва́шего до́ма.
   > Our house is newer **than your house**.

   >   nom.   gen.
   > 2'. Он ста́рше меня́.
   > He is older **than I am**.

b. **чем may be used in any situation**. It can be used when comparing nouns or pronouns in any gender, case, and number or with any part of speech that can be compared (e.g., infinitives, adverbs, adjectives, etc.).

Note: In this construction, the second part of the comparison will be in the same case or form as the first part of the comparison.

nom.   nom.

1'. Наш дом нове́е, **чем** ваш дом.
Our house in newer **than** your house.

infinitive   infinitive

2'. Чита́ть по-ру́сски ле́гче, **чем** говори́ть.
Reading Russian is easier **than** speaking it.

prep.   prep.

3'. В Ки́еве тепле́е, **чем** в Москве́.
It's warmer in Kiev **than** in Moscow.

2. "**much**" more, "**much**" better (p. 277)

Use the non-changing form **гора́здо** to express the intensifier "much" with comparatives.

 a. Э́тот дом **гора́здо** бо́льше, чем тот дом.
This house is **much** larger than that one.

 b. Она́ говори́т по-ру́сски **гора́здо** лу́чше, чем я.
She speaks Russian **much** better than I do.

3. The Phrases **just as . . . as** and **not as . . . as** with Adjectives (p. 277)

Use a form of **тако́й** in the same gender, case, and number as the adjective it modifies and join the comparison with the indeclinable word **как** (as). Add the particle **же** after **тако́й** in positive statements.

Remember to keep the adjectives/special modifiers on both sides of the comparison in the same gender, case, and number.

 a. Моя́ маши́н<u>а</u> так<u>а́я</u> же дорог<u>а́я</u>, как тво<u>я́</u>.
My car is **just as expensive as** yours.

 b. Э́тот рома́н (#) не тако́<u>й</u> интере́сн<u>ый</u>, как тот (#).
This novel is not **as interesting as** that one.

4. The Phrases **just as . . . as** and **not as . . . as** with Adverbs (p. 277)

Use a form of the indeclinable word **так** to modify adverbs and join the comparison with the indeclinable word **как** (as). Add the particle **же** after **так** in positive statements.

a. Зимо́й здесь **так же тепло́, как** на Чёрном мо́ре.
It's **just as warm** here in the winter **as** on the Black Sea.

b. Пробежа́ть ми́лю не **так тру́дно, как** проплы́ть ми́лю.
It's not **as hard** to run a mile **as** it is to swim a mile.

5. The Phrase **the (comparative) . . . the (comparative)** (p. 278)

Place **чем** before the first comparative and **тем** before the second comparative.

a. **Чем** <u>ме́ньше</u> ты бу́дешь говори́ть, **тем** <u>лу́чше</u>.
The <u>less</u> you say, the <u>better</u>.

b. **Чем** <u>скоре́е</u> они́ приду́т, **тем** <u>веселе́е</u> он бу́дет.
The <u>sooner</u> they get here, the <u>happier</u> he will be.

6. The Phrase **as . . . as possible** (p. 278)

Use the expression **как мо́жно** plus a simple comparative adjective.

a. Приходи́ сюда́ **как мо́жно** <u>скоре́е</u>.
Get here **as** <u>soon</u> **as possible**.

b. Купи́ маши́ну **как мо́жно** <u>деше́вле</u>.
Buy the car **as** <u>cheaply</u> **as possible**.

III. Превосхо́дная сте́пень—The Superlative Degree

In English, there are primarily two ways to create the superlative forms of adjectives. 1) The **simple superlative** is a one-word form that adds the suffix -**est** to the positive degree of the adjective: new → new**est**. 2) The **compound superlative** is a two-word form that uses the word "most" plus the positive form of the adjective: interesting → **most** interesting. **Note** that adjectives in English form superlatives using one of these models or the other, not both. For example, we do not say "most new" or "interestingest."

In Russian, adjectives also form simple and compound superlatives, but the difference is that **some adjectives can form both types of superlative**. The **simple** superlative adds an ending to the stem of the positive form of the adjective: но́вый → нове́йший; гро́мкий → громча́йший. The **compound** superlative uses the auxiliary word **са́мый** (most) plus the positive form of the adjective: но́вый → **са́мый** но́вый; гро́мкий → **са́мый** гро́мкий.

Unlike the comparative, however, the two forms of the superlative have slightly different meanings. The compound form of the superlative has a comparative shading. **Са́мая интере́сная кни́га** means "the most interesting book" compared to a larger group (for example, those in the library or in a class). The simple superlative, such as **интере́снейшая кни́га**, means "a most interesting book" (p. 279). In other words, it emphasizes that the book is extremely interesting but does not imply that it is **the** most interesting book in a larger group. The simple superlative is formed from a restricted number of adjectives and is used mostly in writing.

A. The Compound Superlative (p. 278)

1. **Formation:** Place the proper form of the word **са́мый** (most) before the positive degree of the adjective.

2. **Use:** Compound superlatives can be used in any gender, case, and number. **са́мый** will always decline in the same gender, case, and number as the positive form of the adjective that it modifies.

a. Э́то са́мый но́вый дом (#) на у́лице.
This is **the newest house** on the street.

b. Я чита́л э́то в са́мой ста́рой кни́ге в мое́й библиоте́ке.
I read this in **the oldest book** in my library.

c. Моро́зова — са́мый интере́сный профе́ссор (#) в университе́те.
Morozova is **the most interesting professor** in the university.

d. Они́ говоря́т с са́мым лу́чшим студе́нтом в кла́ссе.
They are talking with **the best student** in the class.

B. The Simple Superlative (p. 279)

1. **Formation:** Simple superlatives use one of two endings.

a. **-а́йший:** If the final consonant of the adjective stem is **к, г, х** (but not **т** or **д** as with the simple comparative), the ending of the simple superlative is -а́йший (**note** that the **a** is always stressed) and the final consonant of the stem will undergo an alternation: **к → ч, г → ж, х → ш.**

| 1'. высо́кий | → высоча́йший | 3'. стро́гий | → строжа́йший |
| 2'. лёгкий | → легча́йший | 4'. ти́хий | → тиша́йший |

b. **-ейший:** If the final consonant of the stem is **anything other than к, г, or х**, the ending of the simple superlative is -е́йший and the final consonant does not undergo a change.

| 1'. бы́стрый | → быстре́йший | 3'. си́льный | → сильне́йший |
| 2'. но́вый | → нове́йший | 4'. тёплый | → тепле́йший |

2. **Use:** Since both forms of the simple superlative end in full adjective endings, they may be used in any gender, case, and number. (**Remember:** The simple superlative is formed from a limited number of adjectives and is used mostly in writing.)

a. Мы говори́м об интере́снейшей кни́ге.
We are talking about **a most interesting book**.

b. Они́ лю́бят нове́йшую му́зыку.
They like **the latest music**.

C. Creating Superlatives from Simple Comparatives (p. 279)

Simple comparatives, which end in -e or -ee, have the meaning of a superlative when they are followed by the word **всего́** (when referring to things) or **всех** (when referring to people). This is the only way to form the superlatives of adverbs.

1. Чего́ вы хоти́те **бо́льше всего́**? What do you want **most of all**?

2. Ме́ган говори́т по-ру́сски **лу́чше всех**.
Megan speaks Russian **the best of all**.

3. Я его́ люблю́ **бо́льше всех**. I like him **best of all**.

D. How to Express "**the best**" and "**the worst**" (pp. 278–79)

1. In Russian, "**the best**" is **са́мый хоро́ший, лу́чший**, or, for emphasis, **са́мый лу́чший**.

a. Лари́са **са́мая хоро́шая** студе́нтка в кла́ссе.
Larisa is **the best** student in the class.

b. У неё **лу́чшие** отме́тки. She has **the best** grades.

c. Э́то мой **са́мый лу́чший** друг. This is my **very best** friend.

2. In Russian, "**the worst**" is **са́мый плохо́й, ху́дший**, or, for emphasis, **са́мый ху́дший**.

a. Э́то моя́ **са́мая плоха́я** отме́тка в э́том семе́стре.
This is my **worst** grade this semester.

b. Он за́нял **ху́дшее** ме́сто в аудито́рии.
He took **the worst** seat in the lecture hall.

c. Она́ мой **са́мый ху́дший** враг. She is my (**very**) **worst** enemy.

Склоне́ние прилага́тельных: приме́ры
Adjectives: Sample Declensions

I. Hard Stems (p. 349)

Case	Masculine	Neuter	Feminine	Plural
Nominative	но́вый	но́вое	но́вая	но́вые
Accusative	но́вый/-ого	но́вое	но́вую	но́вые/но́вых
Genitive	но́вого		но́вой	но́вых
Prepositional	но́вом		но́вой	но́вых
Dative	но́вому		но́вой	но́вым
Instrumental	но́вым		но́вой	но́выми

II. Soft Stems (p. 349)

Case	Masculine	Neuter	Feminine	Plural
Nominative	си́ний	си́нее	си́няя	си́ние
Accusative	си́ний/-его	си́нее	си́нюю	си́ние/си́них
Genitive	си́него		си́ней	си́них
Prepositional	си́нем		си́ней	си́них
Dative	си́нему		си́ней	си́ним
Instrumental	си́ним		си́ней	си́ними

III. Velar Stems (к, г, х) (p. 349)

Case	Masculine	Neuter	Feminine	Plural
Nominative	ру́сский	ру́сское	ру́сская	ру́сские
Accusative	ру́сский/-ого	ру́сское	ру́сскую	ру́сские/ру́сских
Genitive	ру́сского		ру́сской	ру́сских
Prepositional	ру́сском		ру́сской	ру́сских
Dative	ру́сскому		ру́сской	ру́сским
Instrumental	ру́сским		ру́сской	ру́сскими

IV. Husher Stems (ж, ч, ш, щ) (p. 349)

Case	Masculine	Neuter	Feminine	Plural
Nominative	большо́й[1]	большо́е	больша́я	больши́е
Accusative	большо́й/-о́го	большо́е	большу́ю	больши́е/больши́х
Genitive	большо́го		большо́й	больши́х
Prepositional	большо́м		большо́й	больши́х
Dative	большо́му		большо́й	больши́м
Instrumental	больши́м		большо́й	больши́ми

---

[1] Adjectives with end stress take the ending -о́й (rather than -ый) in the masculine nominative singular.

V. Special Possessive Adjectives (pp. 154–55, 354)

Case	Masculine	Neuter	Feminine	Plural
Nominative	Са́шин (#)	Са́шино	Са́шина	Са́шины
Accusative	Са́шин/-ого	Са́шино	Са́шину	Са́шины/Са́шиных
Genitive	Са́шиного		Са́шиной	Са́шиных
Prepositional	Са́шином		Са́шиной	Са́шиных
Dative	Са́шиному		Са́шиной	Са́шиным
Instrumental	Са́шиным		Са́шиной	Са́шиными

A. Formation and Use

Possessive adjectives can be formed from names and nicknames ending in -a/-**я**, such as Та́ня, Ве́ра, Ма́ша, Ми́тя, Са́ша, and Ва́ня. To form these adjectives, **remove** the ending (-a/-**я**) from the name, **add** the suffix -**ин**-, and then **add** the proper adjective ending. Special possessive adjectives decline just like a **special modifier**: they use short forms in the nominative case and in the accusative case (except when they modify **masculine or plural animate** nouns) and long forms everywhere else. (**See** the chapter "Pronouns and Special Modifiers," section II, in this grammar for a full list of special modifiers and their declensions.)

Name	Stem	Suffix	Adjective Ending	
Са́ша	Са́ш- +	-ин- +	a	= Са́шина

B. Examples

1. Э́то Са́шина сестра́, а э́то Ми́тины роди́тели.
This is **Sasha's** sister, and these are **Mitia's** parents.

2. Мы говори́м о Ве́рином па́рне. We are talking about **Vera's** boyfriend.

3. Они́ благода́рны Та́ниным де́тям. They are grateful to **Tania's** children.

Котóрый—The Relative Pronoun

I. Definition: The relative pronoun serves two roles. First, like other pronouns, it refers to an antecedent. Second, it introduces a subordinate clause. Combining these two functions, the relative pronoun links the subordinate clause it is in to the main clause of its sentence by referring back to an antecedent in the main clause. Relative pronouns in English are "who," "which," and "that." In Russian, **котóрый** is the relative pronoun when the antecedent is a noun.[1]

II. Use: котóрый **declines like an adjective** and therefore can decline in any gender, case, and number; however, you must consider **both** of its functions mentioned in section I above in order to decline it properly (p. 9).

    A. The **gender** and **number** of котóрый are determined by its **antecedent**—the noun that it refers to.

    B. The **case** of котóрый is determined by **how it functions in its own clause**.

III. Examples (pp. 37, 65, 71, 95, 99, 126, 145)

                                   masculine
                masculine   singular
                singular   nominative

A. Я говорю́ о профéссоре, **котóрый** преподаёт ру́сскую литерату́ру.
I am talking about the professor **who** teaches Russian literature.

котóрый is masculine and singular because its antecedent in the main clause (профéссор) is masculine and singular; it is in **nominative case** because it functions as the **subject** of its own clause.

                          feminine
             feminine   singular
             singular   accusative

B. Вот идёт студéнтка, **котóрую** я ви́дел на вечери́нке.
Here comes the student **that (whom)** I saw at the party.

котóрую is feminine and singular because the noun it refers back to in the main clause (студéнтка) is feminine and singular; it is **accusative** because it is the **direct object** of the verb ви́дел in its own clause.

                               masculine
              masculine   singular
             singular   dative

C. Ивáн Петрóвич говори́т с мои́м врачóм, к **котóрому** я вчерá ходи́л.
Ivan Petrovich is talking with my doctor, **whom** I went to see yesterday.

котóрому is masculine and singular because врач is masculine and singular; it is **dative** because it is the object of the preposition **к** in its own clause.

---

[1] Кто and что are used as relative pronouns when the antecedent is a pronoun.

                        plural
        plural   genitive

D. Мои́ тётя и дя́дя, у **кото́рых** я живу́ ле́том, рабо́тают в университе́те.
My aunt and uncle, with **whom** I live in the summer, work at the university.

кото́рых is plural because it refers to a plural antecedent (тётя и дя́дя); it is in **genitive case** because it is the object of the preposition **у** in its own clause.

                      neuter
        neuter   singular
        singular   prepositional

E. Ещё стро́ят общежи́тие, в **кото́ром** я бу́ду жить в сле́дующем году́.
They are still building the dormitory **that** I will live in next year.

кото́ром is neuter and singular because its antecedent (общежи́тие) is neuter and singular; it is in **prepositional case** because in its own clause it is the object of the preposition **в**, which here expresses location.

Наре́чия—Adverbs

I. Adverbs Formed from Adjectives

A. Образова́ние—Formation

In Russian, adverbs can be formed from most adjectives. **Remove** the adjective ending to get the stem of the adverb, and **add** the proper ending.

1. **Adjectives ending in -ский/-цкий** form adverbs with the ending **-и.**

Adjective		Adverb
a. истори́**ческий** (historic[al])	→	истори́чес**ки** (historical**ly**)
b. геро́й**ский** (heroic)	→	геро́й**ски** (heroical**ly**)

2. **Other adjectives** form adverbs with **the ending -o.**

Adjective		Adverb
a. хоро́ший (good)	→	хорошо́ (**well**)
b. све́тлый (bright)	→	светло́ (bright**ly**)
c. прия́тный (pleasant)	→	прия́тно (pleasant**ly**)

B. Употребле́ние—Use: Adverbs answer the question Как? (How?).

1. **Как** ди́ктор говори́л? Он говори́л сли́шком бы́стро и гро́мко.
How was the announcer speaking? He was speaking too **fast** and too loud**ly**.

2. **Как** Та́ня игра́ет на скри́пке? Она́ **хорошо́** игра́ет.
How does Tania play the violin? She plays it **well**.

II. Remember These Adverbs of Place (p. 23)

A. Question:

Location	Destination	Point of Departure/Origin
Где он?	**Куда́** она́ идёт?	**Отку́да** они́ иду́т?

B. Answer:

Location	Destination	Point of Departure/Origin
1. Он **здесь.** He is **here.**	Она́ идёт **сюда́.** She is coming **here.**	Они́ иду́т **отсю́да.** They are coming **from here.**
2. Он **там.** He is **there.**	Она́ идёт **туда́.** She is going **there.**	Они́ иду́т **отту́да.** They are coming **from there.**
3. Он **до́ма.** He is (**at**) **home.**	Она́ идёт **домо́й.** She is going **home.**	Они́ иду́т **из до́ма** (**и́з дому**). They are coming **from home.**

118

Коли́чественные числи́тельные—Cardinal Numerals

I. The Numeral "One" (1)

A. Склоне́ние—Declension (p. 348)

The numeral "one" declines like a special modifier:[1] it uses short forms in the nominative case and in the accusative case (except when it modifies **masculine or plural animate** nouns) and long forms everywhere else.

Case	Masculine	Neuter	Feminine	Plural
Nominative	оди́н (#)	одно́	одна́	одни́
Accusative	оди́н/одно́го	одно́	одну́	одни́/одни́х
Genitive	одно́го		одно́й	одни́х
Prepositional	одно́м		одно́й	одни́х
Dative	одному́		одно́й	одни́м
Instrumental	одни́м		одно́й	одни́ми

B. Употребле́ние—Use (pp. 93, 95, 100)

The numeral "one" (and any cardinal numeral with the last digit of "one" [this excludes 11]) **does not change the case of the nouns and adjectives it modifies but rather always agrees in gender, case, and number with the noun it modifies.** Nouns and adjectives modified by a numeral ending with the digit "one" are singular.

1. В на́шем кла́ссе два́дцать оди́н (#) ру́сск**ий** ма́льчик (#). (masc. nom. sg.)
There are twenty-one Russian boys in our class.

2. Я говорю́ об одн**о́й** но́в**ой** ру́сск**ой** студе́нтк**е**. (feminine locative sg.)
I'm talking about the one new Russian student.

II. The Numerals 2, 3, 4

A. Склоне́ние—Declension (p. 369)

Case	два	три	четы́ре
Nominative	два/две[2]	три	четы́ре
Accusative	два/две/двух	три/трёх	четы́ре/четырёх
Genitive	двух	трёх	четырёх
Prepositional	двух	трёх	четырёх
Dative	двум	трём	четырём
Instrumental	двумя́	тремя́	четырьмя́

B. Употребле́ние—Use: Nominative and Accusative Case (pp. 93, 95, 100)

When 2, 3, 4—or any compound numeral with the last digit of 2, 3, or 4 (this excludes 12, 13, and 14)—are in nominative or accusative case, the **nouns** they modify go into the **genitive singular.** Any **adjectives** modifying these nouns go into the **genitive plural** (for masculine and neuter nouns) or **nominative plural** (for feminine nouns). **The one exception is when 2, 3, or 4 modify an animate noun in the accusative.** In these

---

[1] **See** the chapter "Pronouns and Special Modifiers," section II, in this grammar.
[2] два is used with masculine and neuter nouns; две is used with feminine nouns.

instances, the accusative/genitive form of the numeral is used (двух, трёх, четырёх), and all adjectives and nouns that it modifies are in the accusative/genitive (animate) plural.

1. **Имени́тельный паде́ж—Nominative Case**

nom. gen. pl. gen. sg.
a. Во дворе́ стоя́ли два ру́сских учи́теля. (учи́тель is masculine)
Two Russian teachers were standing in the courtyard.

nom. nom. nom. pl. gen. sg.
b. В саду́ два́дцать две ру́сские же́нщины. (же́нщина is feminine)
Twenty-two Russian women are in the garden.

2. **Вини́тельный паде́ж—Accusative Case (with inanimate nouns)**

acc. gen. pl. gen. sg.
a. Я чита́ю два но́вых журна́ла. (журна́л is masculine)
I am reading two new magazines.

acc. nom. pl. gen. sg.
b. Я купи́ла две но́вые кни́ги. (кни́га is feminine)
I bought two new books.

3. **But** for **animate** nouns after 2, 3, or 4 in the accusative case:

acc./gen. acc./gen. pl. acc./gen. pl.
a. Я ви́жу **двух** ру́сских студе́нтов. (animate noun)
I see two Russian students.

acc./gen. acc./gen. pl. acc./gen. pl.
b. Я ви́жу **трёх** ру́сских же́нщин (#). (animate noun)
I see three Russian women.

III. The Numerals 5–20

A. **Склоне́ние—Declension:** These numerals decline like дверь-type nouns (p. 369).[3]

Case	пять	во́семь	шестна́дцать	два́дцать
Nominative	пять (#)	во́семь (#)	шестна́дцать (#)	два́дцать (#)
Accusative	пять (#)	во́семь (#)	шестна́дцать (#)	два́дцать (#)
Genitive	пяти́	восьми́	шестна́дцати	двадцати́
Prepositional	пяти́	восьми́	шестна́дцати	двадцати́
Dative	пяти́	восьми́	шестна́дцати	двадцати́
Instrumental	пятью́	восьмью́	шестна́дцатью	двадцатью́

B. **Употребле́ние—Use: Nominative and Accusative Case** (pp. 94, 95, 100)

When 5–20 (or any numeral with the last digit of 5, 6, 7, 8, 9, or 0) are in nominative or accusative case, **all nouns and adjectives** that come after them are in **genitive plural**.

---

[3] The nominative forms of cardinal numerals are spelled with only one soft sign. For numerals 30 and below the soft sign is at the end of the word; for 50, 60, 70, and 80 it is in the middle.

1. Имени́тельный паде́ж—Nominative Case

nom.   gen. pl.   gen. pl.

a. В кла́ссе сиде́ло пять **но́вых студе́нтов**.
Five new students were sitting in class.

nom.   gen. pl.   gen. pl.

b. На стадио́не бе́гали три́дцать **ру́сских спортсме́нок** (#).
Thirty Russian women athletes were running in the stadium.

2. Вини́тельный паде́ж—Accusative Case

acc.   gen. pl.   gen. pl.

a. Я до́лжен прочита́ть де́сять **ру́сских рома́нов**.
I have to read ten Russian novels.

acc.   gen. pl.   gen. pl

b. Я ви́жу на у́лице семь **ру́сских мужчи́н** (#).
I see seven Russian men on the street.

IV. Роди́тельный, предло́жный, да́тельный и твори́тельный падежи́—When Cardinal Numerals are in Genitive, Prepositional, Dative, or Instrumental Case

A. Употребле́ние—Use

When any numeral (except for numerals ending in "one") up to 999 (for example, 2, 5, 17, 36, 90, 100, 748, 911) is in one of these cases, **all adjectives and nouns that it modifies are in the same case as the numeral and plural**. Finally common sense and agreement prevail!!! For numerals with the last digit of "1" (this excludes 11), all adjectives and nouns that they modify are in the same case as the numeral and **singular**.

B. Приме́ры—Examples

genitive   gen. sg.   gen. sg.   gen. sg.

1. Я получи́ла пи́сьма от двадцати́ **одного́ ру́сского дру́га**. (от + gen. case)
I received letters from twenty-one Russian friends.

dative   dative pl.   dative pl.

2. Я позвони́ла двум **ру́сским учителя́м**. (позвони́ть + dative case)
I telephoned the two Russian teachers.

instrumental   instr.   instr. pl.   instr. pl.

3. Я дово́лен двадцатью́ пятью́ **но́выми студе́нтами**. (дово́лен + instr. case)
I am satisfied with the twenty-five new students.

prepositional   prep.   prep. pl.   prep. pl.

4. Я говорю́ о пяти́десяти[4] двух **ру́сских строи́телях**. (о + prep. case)
I am talking about the fifty-two Russian construction workers.

---

[4] For the declension of 50, 60, 70, and 80, **see** the following chapter, "Review: The Declension of Numerals," section III, in this grammar.

Review: The Declension of Numerals

I. The Numeral "One" (1): See the previous chapter, "Cardinal Numerals," section I, A.

II. The Numerals 2, 3, 4: See the previous chapter, "Cardinal Numerals," section II, A.

III. The Numerals 5–20; 30, 50, 60, 70, 80: For the declension of the numerals 5–20, **see** the previous chapter, "Cardinal Numerals," section III, A. In addition, the numerals thirty (три́дцать), fifty (пятьдеся́т), sixty (шестьдеся́т), seventy (се́мьдесят), and eighty (во́семьдесят) follow this declension, the difference being that both parts of fifty, sixty, seventy, and eighty decline.[1] (pp. 369, 370)

Case	30	50	60	80
Nominative	три́дцать (#)	пятьдеся́т (#)	шестьдеся́т (#)	во́семьдесят (#)
Accusative	три́дцать (#)	пятьдеся́т (#)	шестьдеся́т (#)	во́семьдесят (#)
Genitive	тридцати́	пяти́десяти	шести́десяти	восьми́десяти
Prepositional	тридцати́	пяти́десяти	шести́десяти	восьми́десяти
Dative	тридцати́	пяти́десяти	шести́десяти	восьми́десяти
Instrumental	тридцатью́	пятью́десятью	шестью́десятью	восьмью́десятью

IV. 40, 90, 100 (p. 369)

Case	40	90	100
Nominative	со́рок (#)	девяно́сто	сто
Accusative	со́рок (#)	девяно́сто	сто
Genitive	сорока́	девяно́ста	ста
Prepositional	сорока́	девяно́ста	ста
Dative	сорока́	девяно́ста	ста
Instrumental	сорока́	девяно́ста	ста

V. 200, 300, 400: Both parts of the number decline. For a review of the declension of **2, 3**, and **4, see** the previous chapter, "Cardinal Numerals," section II, A. **сто** declines like a neuter noun with a fill vowel. In the nominative and accusative cases it takes a genitive singular ending (**note** the exceptional form двéсти); in all other cases it takes the plural ending of the case it is in: no ending (-#) in genitive, -**ах** in prepositional, -**ам** in dative, and -**ами** in instrumental. (p. 370)

Case	200	300	400
Nominative	две́сти	три́ста	четы́реста
Accusative	две́сти	три́ста	четы́реста
Genitive	двухсо́т (#)	трёхсо́т (#)	четырёхсо́т (#)
Prepositional	двухста́х	трёхста́х	четырёхста́х
Dative	двумста́м	трёмста́м	четырёмста́м
Instrumental	двумяста́ми	тремяста́ми	четырьмяста́ми

VI. 500–900: Again, both parts of the number decline. 5, 6, 7, 8, and 9 decline like дверь-type nouns (**see** the previous chapter, "Cardinal Numerals," section III, A), and сто declines like a neuter noun with a fill vowel. In the nominative, accusative, and genitive cases сто takes a

---

[1] As with 5–20, there is only one soft sign in these numerals in the nominative case. For 30 it is at the end of the word, just as in 5–20; for 50, 60, 70, and 80 the soft sign is in the middle of the word.

genitive plural ending (-#), and in all other cases it takes the plural ending of the case it is in: **-ax** in prepositional, **-ам** in dative, and **-ами** in instrumental. (p. 370)

Case	500	600	700	800	900
Nominative	пятьсóт (#)	шестьсóт (#)	семьсóт (#)	восемьсóт (#)	девятьсóт (#)
Accusative	пятьсóт (#)	шестьсóт (#)	семьсóт (#)	восемьсóт (#)	девятьсóт (#)
Genitive	пятисóт (#)	шестисóт (#)	семисóт (#)	восьмисóт (#)	девятисóт (#)
Prepositional	пятистáх	шестистáх	семистáх	восьмистáх	девятистáх
Dative	пятистáм	шестистáм	семистáм	восьмистáм	девятистáм
Instrumental	пятьюстáми	шестьюстáми	семьюстáми	восьмьюстáми	девятьюстáми

VII. 1000 declines like a feminine **кни́га**-type noun. **Adjectives and nouns after "ты́сяча" take the genitive plural no matter what case the numeral is in.** (p. 370)

Case	1000
Nominative	ты́сяча
Accusative	ты́сячу
Genitive	ты́сячи
Prepositional	ты́сяче
Dative	ты́сяче
Instrumental	ты́сячей/ты́сячью

VIII. миллиóн (million) and **миллиáрд** (billion) decline like masculine **стол**-type nouns. **Adjectives and nouns after these numerals take the genitive plural no matter what case the numeral is in.** (p. 370)

Note: All parts of a compound numeral decline.

Case	253
Nominative	двéсти пятьдеся́т три
Accusative	двéсти пятьдеся́т три
Genitive	двухсóт пяти́десяти трёх
Prepositional	двухстáх пяти́десяти трёх
Dative	двумстáм пяти́десяти трём
Instrumental	двумястáми пятью́десятью тремя́

IX. Indefinite Numerals (Adverbs of Quantity): ско́лько, мно́го, немно́го, ма́ло, не́сколько

When an indefinite numeral is in the nominative or accusative case . . .

A. put nouns and adjectives into the **genitive singular** after **ско́лько** (how much), **мно́го** (much, a lot), **немно́го** (a little, some, enough to suffice), and **ма́ло** (little, too little, not enough) **for things that cannot be counted** (do not naturally come in units). (pp. 94, 95, 100)

1. ско́лько чи́стой воды́?
how much clean water?

2. мно́го вре́мени
a lot of time

3. ма́ло я́ркого со́лнца
not enough bright sun

4. немно́го рабо́ты
some (a little) work

B. put nouns and adjectives into the **genitive plural** after **ско́лько** (how many), **не́сколько** (several, some, enough to suffice), **мно́го** (a lot, many), **немно́го** (some, enough to suffice), and **ма́ло** (too few, not enough) **for things that can be counted** (do come naturally in units). (pp. 94, 95, 100)

1. ско́лько книг (#)?
how many books?

2. мно́го музе́ев
many museums

3. не́сколько но́вых сту́льев
several new chairs

4. ма́ло ру́сских учителе́й
not enough Russian teachers

C. Use the special genitive plural form **челове́к** (persons) after **ско́лько** and **не́сколько** (and also after numbers that require the genitive plural of this noun: 25 челове́к). Use the regular genitive plural form **люде́й** after **мно́го**, **немно́го**, and **ма́ло**. (p. 94)

1. **Ско́лько** бы́ло **челове́к**? **How many people** were there?
2. Бы́ло **не́сколько челове́к**. There were just **a few people**.
3. Там бы́ло **мно́го люде́й**. There were **a lot of people** there.

X. о́ба/о́бе—"Both" (p. 371)

Case usage for words modified by о́ба/о́бе is the same as for два/две for both adjectives and nouns. See the previous chapter, "Cardinal Numerals," sections II, B, and IV.

Case	Masculine/Neuter	Feminine
Nominative	о́ба	о́бе
Accusative	о́ба/обо́их	о́бе/обе́их
Genitive	обо́их	обе́их
Prepositional	обо́их	обе́их
Dative	обо́им	обе́им
Instrumental	обо́ими	обе́ими

XI. Collective Numerals: дво́е ("two of"), тро́е ("three of"), че́тверо ("four of"), пя́теро, ше́стеро, се́меро, во́сьмеро, де́вятеро, де́сятеро (p. 371)

Use **genitive plural** for both adjectives and nouns modified by collective numerals.

Case	дво́е	тро́е	че́тверо–де́сятеро
Nominative	дво́е	тро́е	че́тверо
Accusative	дво́е/двои́х	тро́е/трои́х	че́тверо/четверы́х
Genitive	двои́х	трои́х	четверы́х
Prepositional	двои́х	трои́х	четверы́х
Dative	двои́м	трои́м	четверы́м
Instrumental	двои́ми	трои́ми	четверы́ми

Note: пя́теро, ше́стеро, се́меро, во́сьмеро, де́вятеро, and де́сятеро take "hard" endings (like че́тверо) throughout their declension.

XII. The Numeral полтора́/полторы́ (one and a half) (p. 371)

Case	Masculine/Neuter	Feminine
Nominative	полтора́	полторы́
Accusative	полтора́	полторы́
Genitive	полу́тора	полу́тора
Prepositional	полу́тора	полу́тора
Dative	полу́тора	полу́тора
Instrumental	полу́тора	полу́тора

XIII. Ordinal Numerals (p. 372)

Cardinal Numeral		Ordinal Numeral	Cardinal Numeral		Ordinal Numeral
1	оди́н	пе́рвый	30	три́дцать	тридца́тый
2	два	второ́й	40	со́рок	сороково́й
3	три	тре́тий	50	пятьдеся́т	пятидеся́тый
4	четы́ре	четвёртый	60	шестьдеся́т	шестидеся́тый
5	пять	пя́тый	70	се́мьдесят	семидеся́тый
6	шесть	шесто́й	80	во́семьдесят	восьмидеся́тый
7	семь	седьмо́й	90	девяно́сто	девяно́стый
8	во́семь	восьмо́й	100	сто	со́тый
9	де́вять	девя́тый	200	две́сти	двухсо́тый
10	де́сять	деся́тый	300	три́ста	трёхсо́тый
11	оди́ннадцать	оди́ннадцатый	400	четы́реста	четырёхсо́тый
12	двена́дцать	двена́дцатый	500	пятьсо́т	пятисо́тый
13	трина́дцать	трина́дцатый	600	шестьсо́т	шестисо́тый
14	четы́рнадцать	четы́рнадцатый	700	семьсо́т	семисо́тый
15	пятна́дцать	пятна́дцатый	800	восемьсо́т	восьмисо́тый
16	шестна́дцать	шестна́дцатый	900	девятьсо́т	девятисо́тый
17	семна́дцать	семна́дцатый	1 000	ты́сяча	ты́сячный
18	восемна́дцать	восемна́дцатый	2 000 две ты́сячи		двухты́сячный
19	девятна́дцать	девятна́дцатый	1 000 000	миллио́н	миллио́нный
20	два́дцать	двадца́тый	1 000 000 000	миллиа́рд	миллиа́рдный

Note: In compound ordinal numerals, the only part to decline like an adjective begins with the last digit that is not a zero and includes any zeroes that follow it. All other digits remain cardinal numerals and do not decline. This is the same as in English: the **twentieth** day; the twenty-**first** day; the two thousand five hundred and **sixtieth** customer, the two thousand five hundred and sixty-**seventh** customer.

20[th] = двадца́тый

21[st] = два́дцать **пе́рвый**

200[th] = **двухсо́тый**

201[st] = две́сти **пе́рвый**

2,567[th] = две ты́сячи пятьсо́т шестьдеся́т **седьмо́й**

в 2000 году́ = в **двухты́сячном** году́

в 2005 году́ = в две ты́сячи **пя́том** году́

Вре́мя по часа́м—Clock Time

Just as in English, Russian distinguishes between the questions "**What time is it?**"—Кото́рый час? or Ско́лько вре́мени?—and "**When?**" or "**At What Time?**"—Когда́? Во ско́лько? В кото́ром часу́?

Note: The twenty-four-hour clock is used in official schedules (pp. 33, 42).

I. Time on the Hour

A. **Кото́рый час? Ско́лько вре́мени?** (What time is it?) (p. 42)

1. The answer places a **cardinal numeral** in **nominative case** with the word **час** (here meaning "o'clock") in **genitive singular after 2, 3,** and **4** and in **genitive plural after 5–12**. "One o'clock" is rendered as "**час**" (in accusative case without the special modifier оди́н).

2. Кото́рый час? Ско́лько сейча́с вре́мени? Сейча́с . . .

    a. час (**#**). = It's one o'clock. (**Note** that the numeral "one" is omitted.)

    b. два (три, четы́ре) часа́. = It's two (three, four) o'clock.

    c. пять (шесть, семь, во́семь, де́вять, . . . двена́дцать) часо́в. = It's five (six, seven, eight, nine, . . . twelve) o'clock.

    d. по́лдень (**#**). = It's noon; по́лночь (**#**). = It's midnight.

B. **Когда́? Во ско́лько? В кото́ром часу́?** (When? At what time?) (p. 42)

1. The answer "at" a given hour is rendered in Russian by the preposition **в** + a **cardinal numeral in accusative case** + the word **час** in **genitive singular after 2, 3,** and **4** and in **genitive plural after 5–12**. "At one o'clock" is rendered as "**в час**" (in accusative case without the special modifier оди́н).

2. Когда́ (Во ско́лько/В кото́ром часу́) они́ пришли́? Они́ пришли́ . . .

    a. в час (**#**). = **at** one o'clock (**Note** that the numeral "one" is omitted.)

    b. в два (три, четы́ре) часа́. = **at** two (three, four) o'clock

    c. в пять (шесть, семь, во́семь, де́вять, де́сять и т.д.) часо́в. = **at** five (six, seven, eight, nine, ten, etc.) o'clock

    d. в по́лдень (**#**). = **at** noon; в по́лночь (**#**). = **at** midnight

C. Expressing "**up to/before**," "**about/around**," "**after**," and "**since/from**" (p. 43)

1. The Prepositions

    a. **до** = up to, before   c. **по́сле** = after
    b. **о́коло** = about, around   d. **с** = since, from

2. Since each of the above prepositions governs the genitive case, the **cardinal numerals that follow them must be in genitive case**, and the word for "o'clock" (**час**) must be in **genitive plural, except in the case of 1, which is rendered in the genitive singular without the special modifier "one" simply as "ча́са."**

a. Склоне́ние—Declension

You only need to know the genitive case of the numerals 2–12 for this time expression. If you wish to consult the complete declensions of these numerals, **see** the chapter "Cardinal Numerals," sections II, A, and III, A, in this grammar. **Note:** 5–12 decline like дверь-type nouns.

1'. two, three, four = двух, трёх, четырёх

2'. five–twelve = пяти́, шести́, семи́, восьми́, девяти́, десяти́, оди́ннадцати, двена́дцати

b. Приме́ры—Examples

1'. Они́ рабо́тали **до** ча́са.[1] They worked **until one**.
2'. Она́ ви́дела его́ **о́коло двух.** She saw him **around two**.
3'. Ле́кция начала́сь **по́сле** пяти́. The lecture began **after five**.

D. Expressing "**from**" a given hour "**to**" a given hour is rendered with the prepositions **с** (from) and **до** (to). Since both these prepositions govern genitive case, the **cardinal numerals that follow them must be in genitive case**, and the word for "o'clock" (**час**) must be in **genitive plural, except in the case of 1, which is rendered in the genitive singular without the special modifier "one" simply as "ча́са."** (p. 44)

1. Они́ занима́лись с ча́су[1] до пяти́. They studied <u>from</u> **one** <u>until</u> **five**.
2. Мы рабо́тали с **двух** до восьми́. We worked <u>from</u> **two** <u>to</u> **eight**.
3. Бо́ря был у нас с десяти́ до **трёх.** Boria was at our place <u>from</u> **ten** <u>to</u> **three**.

E. **Approximate time** is expressed by reversing the numeral and the word for "o'clock" (p. 44).

1. де́сять часо́в = ten o'clock   часо́в де́сять = **about** ten o'clock
2. до двух часо́в = until two o'clock   часо́в до двух = until **about** two o'clock

II. Time on the Half Hour (p. 72)

Note: For clock time **other than on the hour**, Russians express time as how much of the **upcoming** hour has elapsed. Thus, 12:30 is "полови́на пе́рвого" (half of **one** o'clock).

A. Кото́рый час? Ско́лько вре́мени? (What time is it?)

1. The answer places the word for "half" (**полови́на**) in **nominative case** with the word for the upcoming hour expressed as an **ordinal numeral** in **genitive singular**.

---

[1] час also *has the* alternate genitive singular form **ча́су**, which can be used after prepositions.

2. Кото́рый час? Ско́лько сейча́с вре́мени? Сейча́с . . .

полови́на пе́рвого (второ́го, тре́тьего, четвёртого, пя́того, шесто́го, седьмо́го, восьмо́го, девя́того, деся́того, оди́ннадцатого, двена́дцатого).[2] =

12:30 (1:30, 2:30, 3:30, etc.) or half past twelve (half past one, etc.)

В. Когда́? Во ско́лько? В кото́ром часу́? (When? At what time?)

1. The answer places the word for "half" (**полови́на**) in **locative case** after the preposition **в** with the word for the upcoming hour expressed as an **ordinal numeral** in the **genitive singular**.

2. Когда́ (Во ско́лько/В кото́ром часу́) они́ пришли́? Они́ пришли́ . . .

в полови́не пе́рвого (второ́го, тре́тьего, четвёртого и т.д.).[3] =
at 12:30 (1:30, 2:30, 3:30, etc.) or **at** half past twelve (half past one, etc.)

III. Time in the First Half of the Hour (1 minute to 30 minutes **after** the hour) (pp. 72–73)

Note: For clock time **other than on the hour,** Russians express time as how much of the **upcoming** hour has elapsed. Thus, 12:20 is "два́дцать мину́т пе́рвого" (twenty minutes into the **first** hour [**one** o'clock]).

А. Кото́рый час? Ско́лько вре́мени? (What time is it?)

1. The answer places the **cardinal numerals 1–30 in nominative case** with the word for "minutes" (**мину́та**) in the proper case after numerals in nominative case: **nominative after 1 and 21; genitive singular after 2, 3, 4 and 22, 23, 24;** and **genitive plural after 5–20 and 25–30.** As with time on the half hour, the upcoming hour is expressed as an **ordinal numeral** in **genitive singular.**

2. Кото́рый час? Ско́лько сейча́с вре́мени? Сейча́с . . .

a. minutes with the last digit of "**one**"

1'. одна́ мину́та пе́рвого. = 12:01 (one minute into the first hour)
2'. одна́ мину́та второ́го. = 1:01
3'. два́дцать одна́ мину́та тре́тьего. = 2:21

b. minutes with the last digit of "**two**," "**three**," or "**four**"

1'. две мину́ты пя́того. = 4:02 (two minutes into the fifth hour)
2'. три мину́ты шесто́го. = 5:03
3'. два́дцать четы́ре мину́ты седьмо́го. = 6:24

---

[2] This phrase can be shortened into one word by combining the fragment **пол** with the ordinal numeral. Thus, полпе́рвого = 12:30, полвторо́го = 1:30, etc.

[3] This phrase can be shortened into one word by combining the fragment **пол** with the ordinal numeral. Thus, полпе́рвого = **at** 12:30, полвторо́го = **at** 1:30, etc.

c. the minutes **5–20** and **25–30**

> 1'. пять мину́т (#) девя́**того**. = 8:05
> (five minutes into the ninth hour)
>
> 2'. де́сять мину́т (#) деся́**того**. = 9:10
> 3'. пятна́дцать мину́т (#) оди́ннадцат**ого**. = 10:15
> 4'. два́дцать пять мину́т (#) двена́дцат**ого**. = 11:25

d. **"quarter"** past the hour is rendered by the word **"че́тверть."**

> 1'. че́тверть тре́ть**его**. = 2:15 (one quarter into the third hour)
> 2'. че́тверть девя́**того**. = 8:15
> 3'. че́тверть оди́ннадцат**ого**. = 10:15

B. **Когда́? Во ско́лько? В кото́ром часу́?** (When? At what time?)

1. The answer places the **cardinal numerals 1–30** in **accusative case** with the word for "minutes" (**мину́та**) in the proper case after numerals in accusative case: **accusative after 1 and 21; genitive singular after 2, 3, 4 and 22, 23, 24; and genitive plural after 5–20 and 25–30.** As with time on the half hour, the upcoming hour is expressed as an **ordinal numeral** in **genitive singular.**

Note: The use of the preposition **в** in this type of time expression is optional.

2. Когда́ (Во ско́лько/В кото́ром часу́) они́ пришли́? Они́ пришли́ . . .

a. minutes with the last digit of **"one"**

> 1'. (**в**) одну́ мину́ту пе́рв**ого**. = **at** 12:01
> (at one minute into the first hour)
>
> 2'. (**в**) одну́ мину́ту втор**о́го**. = **at** 1:01
> 3'. (**в**) одну́ мину́ту тре́ть**его**. = **at** 2:01
> 4'. (**в**) два́дцать одну́ мину́ту четвёрт**ого**. = **at** 3:21

b. minutes with the last digit of **"two," "three,"** or **"four"**

> 1'. (**в**) две мину́**ты** пя́**того**. = **at** 4:02
> (at two minutes into the fifth hour)
>
> 2'. (**в**) три мину́**ты** шест**о́го**. = **at** 5:03
> 3'. (**в**) четы́ре мину́**ты** седьм**о́го**. = **at** 6:04
> 4'. (**в**) два́дцать четы́ре мину́**ты** восьм**о́го**. = **at** 7:24

c. the minutes **5–20** and **25–30**

> 1'. (**в**) пять мину́т (#) девя́**того**. = **at** 8:05
> (at five minutes into the ninth hour)
>
> 2'. (**в**) де́сять мину́т (#) деся́**того**. = **at** 9:10
> 3'. (**в**) пятна́дцать мину́т (#) оди́ннадцат**ого**. = **at** 10:15
> 4'. (**в**) два́дцать пять мину́т (#) двена́дцат**ого**. = **at** 11:25

d. At "**quarter**" past the hour is rendered by the word "**че́тверть.**"

> 1'. (**в**) че́тверть (#) тре́т**ьего.** = **at** 2:15
> (at one quarter into the third hour)
>
> 2'. (**в**) че́тверть (#) девя́т**ого.** = **at** 8:15
> 3'. (**в**) че́тверть (#) оди́ннадцат**ого.** = **at** 10:15

IV. Time in the Second Half of the Hour (29 minutes to 1 minute **before** the hour) (pp. 73–74)

Note: For clock time **other than on the hour**, Russians express time as how much of the **upcoming** hour has elapsed. Thus, 12:45 is "без пятна́дцати час" (**one** o'clock less [without] fifteen minutes).

A. **Кото́рый час? Ско́лько сейча́с вре́мени?** (What time is it?)

1. The answer places the **cardinal numerals 1–29** in **genitive case after** the prepositon **без**, generally with the word for "minute" (мину́та) given only after the numerals 1, 2, 3, and 4. The **upcoming hour** is rendered as a **cardinal numeral in nominative case.** Generally no word for "o'clock" is given, but "one o'clock" is rendered simply as "час" without the special modifier оди́н.

2. **Склоне́ние—Declension** Here are the genitive forms of the cardinal numerals you will need for this construction. **Remember** that the numerals 5–20 and the word for "quarter" (че́тверть) decline like дверь-type nouns.

> a. two, three, four = двух, трёх, четырёх
>
> b. five–twenty = пяти́, шести́, семи́, восьми́, девяти́, десяти́, оди́ннадцати, двена́дцати трина́дцати, четы́рнадцати . . . , двадцати́
>
> c. one quarter = че́тверти

3. **Кото́рый час? Ско́лько сейча́с вре́мени?** Сейча́с . . .

> a. minutes with the last digit of "**one**"
>
> > 1'. без одно́й мину́ты час. = 12:59
> > (one o'clock less one minute)
> >
> > 2'. без одно́й мину́ты два. = 1:59
> > 3'. без одно́й мину́ты три. = 2:59
> > 4'. без двадцати́ одно́й мину́ты четы́ре. = 3:39
>
> b. minutes with the last digit of "**two**," "**three**," or "**four**"
>
> > 1'. без **двух** мину́т (#) пя́ть. = 4:58
> > (five o'clock less two minutes)
> >
> > 2'. без **трёх** мину́т (#) шесть. = 5:57
> > 3'. без **четырёх** мину́т (#) семь. = 6:56
> > 4'. без двадцати́ **четырёх** мину́т (#) во́семь. = 7:36

c. the minutes **5–20** and **25–29**

    1'. без пяти́ де́вять. = 8:55 (nine o'clock less five minutes)
    2'. без пятна́дцати оди́ннадцать. = 10:45
    3'. без двадцати́ пяти́ двена́дцать. = 11:35

d. **quarter** to the hour

    1'. без че́тверти три. = 2:45 (three o'clock less fifteen minutes)
    2'. без че́тверти де́вять. = 8:45
    3'. без че́тверти оди́ннадцать. = 10:45

B. Когда́? Во ско́лько? В кото́ром ча́су? (When? At what time?)

Note: The grammar for answering the question "When?" or "At what time?" for time in the second half of the hour is exactly the same as the grammar for answering the question "What time is it?" Therefore, the examples in section IV, A, 3, above, apply to this section as well. **The preposition в is not used in this construction.**

V. Expressing A.M. and P.M. (P. 42)

A. Russian expresses this idea by naming the period of the day in the **genitive case**.

    1. но́чи = from midnight until four or five A.M.
    2. утра́ = from four or five A.M. until noon
    3. дня = from noon until five or six P.M.
    4. ве́чера = from five or six P.M. until midnight

B. Приме́ры—Examples

    1. три часа́ **но́чи** = (at) three A.M.
    2. в два́дцать мину́т деся́того **утра́** = at 9:20 A.M.
    3. в полови́не тре́тьего **дня** = at 2:30 P.M.
    4. без пяти́ двена́дцать **ве́чера** = (at) 11:55 P.M.

Expressions of Time Other than Clock Time

This chapter explains how to express time when answering "time questions" such as **Когда́? Как до́лго? Как ча́сто? (На) Ско́лько вре́мени?** and **Како́е сего́дня число́?**

I. The Relationship between Time and Action

You need to distinguish three possible relationships between time and action: 1) the period of time elapses **before** the action takes place (section A, below), 2) the action takes place **some time during** or **throughout** the specified time (section B, below), or 3) the time period begins only **after** the action takes place (section C, below).

   A. Time **before** Action: **че́рез + accusative** (p. 43)

   Когда́?

   1. **Когда́** начну́тся заня́тия? Они́ начну́тся **че́рез** неде́лю.
   When do classes begin? They will begin **in a week.**

                                                                                       acc. gen. sg.
   2. **Когда́** вы пое́дете в Росси́ю? Мы пое́дем в Росси́ю **че́рез два ме́сяца.**[1]
   When are you going to Russia?   We are going to Russia **in two** months.

   B. An Action Takes Place **some time during or throughout** the Specified Time: **accusative case**

   Ско́лько вре́мени?

   1. Use an **imperfective verb** (because the emphasis is on the time spent **doing something** [the action itself] and not a result) **+ accusative case without a preposition** (p. 43).

      a. **Ско́лько вре́мени** Ва́ня рабо́тал над диссерта́цией?
      How long did Vania work on his dissertation?

      b. Он рабо́тал над ней год (#).
      He worked on it **for a year.**[2]

      c. Го́сти из Ита́лии бы́ли у нас неде́лю.
      Our guests from Italy stayed with us **for a week.**[2]

   2. However, if you wish to stress that an action took place over a period of time and **was completed**, use a **perfective verb + за + accusative case** (p. 355).

                                                          acc.   gen. sg.
      a. Мы пригото́вили обе́д **за четы́ре часа́.**
      It took us **four** hours to get dinner ready.

---

[1] To review the use of case with numbers, **see** the chapter "Cardinal Numerals" in this grammar.
[2] **Note** that for this time construction, Russian does not use a preposition to translate the English preposition "for."

> b. Ири́на отве́тила на все пи́сьма за́ день (#).
> Irina answered all the letters **in a day**.

C. Time Begins only **after** the Action Takes Place: **на + accusative case** (pp. 355, 364)

На ско́лько вре́мени?

1. На́ши друзья́ пое́хали в Евро́пу **на** ме́сяц (#).
Our friends have gone to Europe **for a month**.
(After getting to Europe, they are staying for a month.)

2. Я верну́сь **на** час (#). I'll come back **for an hour**.
(After I return, I will stay for an hour.)

II. ка́ждый; весь, це́лый (p. 37)

Each of these words, when used to answer the questions below, modifies a noun in **accusative case**.

A. **ка́ждый** = each, every

Когда́? Как ча́сто?

1. Мы ходи́ли в кино́ ка́ждую суббо́ту.
We went to the movies **every Saturday**.

2. Самолёты прилета́ют ка́ждую мину́ту. Planes are landing **every minute**.

B. **весь** = all, the whole; **це́лый** = a whole, an entire (implies a lot of time for the activity mentioned)

Когда́? Как до́лго?

1. Студе́нты гото́вились к контро́льной весь (#) день (#).
The students studied for the test **all day**.

2. Маши́ну чини́ли це́лую неде́лю. They worked on my car **an entire week**.

III. "Per" Expressions: в + accusative case (p. 38)

This expression is preceded by a numeral or indefinite numeral (ско́лько, не́сколько, мно́го) and the proper form of the word **раз** ("times").

Ско́лько раз?

A. У меня́ курс по ру́сской исто́рии три ра́за **в** неде́лю.
My Russian history course meets three times **per week**.

B. Роди́тели Ма́ши приезжа́ют к нам раз **в** год (#). Masha's parents visit once **a year**.

IV. Days[3]

A. **On** a day of the week is rendered by **в + accusative case** (p. 38).

Когда́? В какóй день? В какúе дни?

1. **В какóй день (#)** ты идёшь к бáбушке? Я идý к ней **в понедéльник (#)**.
When are you going to your grandmother's? I'm going to see her **on Monday**.

2. **В какúе дни** у тебя́ семинáр по литератýре? **В срéду** и **в пя́тницу**.
Which days do you have your literature seminar? **On Wednesday** and **Friday**.

B. **по + dative plural** is used in plural expressions of "on" a certain day of the week and "in" a certain part of the day (p. 31).

Когда́? По какúм дням?

1. Я хожý к бáбушке **по воскресéньям**. I visit my grandmother **on Sundays**.
2. Онá рабóтает **по втóрникам**. She works **(on) Tuesdays**.
3. Я люблю́ занимáться **по вечерáм**. I like to study **in the evenings**.

C. **During** a Part of the Day: **Instrumental Case** (p. 38)

Когда́?

1. Мы рабóтали **ýтром** и отдыхáли **вéчером**.
We worked **in the morning** and rested **in the evening**.

2. Он рабóтает **нóчью**, а спит **днём**.
He works **at night** and sleeps **during the day**.

V. Periods of Time Longer Than a Day[3] (Week, Month, Quarter, Semester, Year; Seasons) (pp. 45–46)

A. Generally, periods of time longer than a day are rendered by **в + prepositional case**.

Когда́? В какóм мéсяце / семéстре / годý? В какóй чéтверти?

1. Нáша грýппа былá в Лóндоне **в мáе / в прóшлом семéстре / в э́том годý**.
Our group was in London **in May / last semester / this year**.[4]

2. Её лéкция бýдет **в э́той чéтверти / в декабрé / в бýдущем годý**.
Her lecture will be **this quarter / in December / next year**.

3. Э́то случúлось **в две ты́сячи трéтьем годý**. This happened **in 2003**.

Note: Years are given as **ordinal numerals**.

---

[3] The prepositions **с** (from) and **до** (to), which are used to express clock time, can also be used with units of time such as days, months, and years to answer the question Когда́?: с понедéльника до средý, с мáя до áвгуста, and с 1971-го года до 1975-го года (p. 364).

[4] Although no preposition is used in the English time phrases "this/last/next month/quarter/semester/year," in Russian **the preposition в + prepositional case** must be used when these phrases answer the question Когда́?

B. One exception to the statement in V, A, above is **неде́ля**, which goes into prepositional case **after the preposition на**.

> ### Когда́? На како́й неде́ле?

> 1. **На** како́й неде́ле ваш экза́мен? **Which week** (of the semester) is your exam?
> 2. Она́ вернётся **на** сле́дующей неде́ле. She is returning **next week**.[5]

C. The **seasons** (зима́, весна́, ле́то, о́сень) are rendered in **instrumental case** (p. 364).

> ### Когда́?

> 1. Мы е́здили в Пари́ж про́шлой весно́й. We went to Paris **last spring**.
> 2. Они́ поже́нятся о́сенью. They are getting married **in the fall**.

VI. Dates

A. Naming Today's, Yesterday's, or Tomorrow's Date (p. 44)

The date is expressed using an **ordinal numeral** in **nominative case**. If the **month** or **year** is added, they are given in **genitive case**, with the year as an ordinal numeral.

> ### Како́е сего́дня число́? Како́е вчера́ бы́ло/за́втра бу́дет число́?

>   nominative genitive
> 1. Како́е сего́дня число́? Сего́дня седьмо́е апре́ля.[6]
> **What** is today's **date**? Today is the **seventh of April**.[7]

>   nom.   gen.
> 2. Вчера́ бы́ло/За́втра бу́дет два́дцать пе́рвое ию́ля.
> Yesterday was/Tomorrow will be the **twenty-first of July**.

B. The Date When Something Occurred (p. 45)

The date is expressed using an **ordinal numeral** in **genitive case**. If the **month** or **year** is added, they are given in **genitive case**. The year is expressed as an ordinal numeral.

> ### Когда́? Како́го числа́?

>   genitive
> 1. Приходи́ к нам шесто́го. Come see us **on the sixth**.[8]

>   genitive   genitive
> 2. Их де́душка прие́хал в Аме́рику тридца́того января́ ты́сяча девятьсо́т
>   genitive
> двена́дцатого го́да. Their grandfather arrived in America **on January 30th, 1912**.

---

[5] Although the English phrases "this/last/next week" are expressed without a preposition, in Russian they must be rendered by **the preposition на + prepositional case** when they answer the question Когда́?

[6] **Remember** that Russians write the day first then the month and year: 7.4.2005 and 7.IV.2005 in Russian = April 7, 2005 (4/7/2005) in English (p. 45).

[7] Just as in English, the word for "date" (число́) is used in Russian in the question but not in the answer.

[8] Russian does not use a preposition to translate the English preposition "on" in this expression.

Частицы -то, -нибудь
The Indefinite Particles -то and -нибудь

Particles are grammatical units that do not function independently; they are used and create meaning in combination with other words (e.g., pronouns, adjectives, and adverbs). (pp. 325–26)

I. Forms

Note: Although the following combinations are translated using the English equivalents of "some-" for the particle -то and "any-" for the particle -нибудь, this is not a hard and fast association. As you will see below in section III, B, the context of the sentence determines the exact translation of these particles. When translating indefinite particles, you need to keep their basic definitions in mind.

A. The Particle -то

кто́-то	someone
что́-то	something
где́-то	somewhere (location)
куда́-то	somewhere (motion)
когда́-то	once, a while ago
како́й-то	some (adjective)
почему́-то	for some reason

B. The Particle -нибудь

кто́-нибудь	anyone, someone
что́-нибудь	anything, something
где́-нибудь	anywhere, somewhere (location)
куда́-нибудь	anywhere, somewhere (motion)
когда́-нибудь	ever, some time in the future
како́й-нибудь	any, some (adjective)

II. Склоне́ние—Declension

A. -то and -нибудь do not decline.

B. где, куда́, когда́, and как do not decline.

C. кто and что decline; **see** the chapter "Pronouns and Special Modifiers," section I, in this grammar for the declensions of кто and что.

D. како́й declines in any gender, case, and number like an adjective with a velar stem (к). (**See** the chapter "Adjectives: Sample Declensions," section III, in this grammar for a detailed chart.)

III. Use

Note: Do not give negative answers using words containing the particles -то and -нибудь. Instead, use negative (ни-) constructions. Use -то and -нибудь only in positive statements.

Кто́-нибудь заходи́л?	Да. **Кто́-то** заходи́л.	Нет. **Никто́** не заходи́л.
Did **anyone** drop by?	Yes. **Someone** did.	No. **No one** dropped by.

Она́ **когда́-нибудь** звони́ла?	Да. Она́ **когда́-то** звони́ла.	Нет. Она́ **никогда́** не звони́ла.
Did she **ever** call?	Yes. She called **a while ago**.	No. She **never** did.

A. **Definitions:** Both of these particles give an **indefinite** meaning to the words they modify. The difference between them is

1. The particle -**нибудь** refers to an entity that may or may not exist or that might be a class of things. It is most often used 1) in **questions** to establish whether or not a particular **кто, что, где, etc.**, exists (examples 1–3 below) or 2) with **imperatives** and the **future tense** of declarative sentences in reference to something non-specific (examples 4–6).

2. The particle -**то** refers to a specific **кто, что, где, etc.**, that exists but is not named. It is most often used in **declarative** sentences with **present** and **past tense** verbs.

B. **Examples**

1. **Кто́-нибудь** приходи́л?
Did **anyone** come by?

(Was there anyone or not?)

1. Да. **Кто́-то** приходи́л.
Yes. **Someone** stopped by.

(A person or persons came by, but the speaker isn't saying or doesn't know who it was.)

2. Они́ **куда́-нибудь** иду́т ве́чером?
Are they going **anywhere** tonight?

(Are they going someplace or not?)

2. Да. Они́ **куда́-то** иду́т.
Yes. They are going **somewhere**.

(They are going somewhere, but the speaker isn't saying or doesn't know where.)

3. Вы **когда́-нибудь** жи́ли в Росси́и?
Have you **ever** lived in Russia?

(Did you ever live in Russia or not?)

3. Да. Я **когда́-то** жила́ в Росси́и.
Yes. I **once** lived in Russia.

(The speaker has lived in Russia but isn't saying when this was.)

4. Я **когда́-нибудь** расскажу́ тебе́ об э́том.
I will tell you about this **someday**.

(It could be any time at all in the future.)

5. Купи́ мне **каку́ю-нибудь** газе́ту.
Buy me **a (any)** newspaper.

(any newspaper at all, it doesn't matter)

6. Расскажи́ **что́-нибудь** о жи́зни в Москве́.
Tell us **something** about life in Moscow.

(whatever you want to, anything at all)

Negative (ни-) Constructions

I. Фóрмы—Forms (p. 212)

A. Negative Constructions

1.	никтó	nobody, no one, none, anybody, anyone
2.	ничтó/ничегó	nothing, anything
3.	нигдé	nowhere, anywhere (location)
4.	никудá	nowhere, anywhere (motion)
5.	никогдá	never
6.	никакóй	no . . . , none, any . . . (adjective)
7.	никáк	by no means, not at all, in no way

B. Склонéние—Declension

1. The adverbs **нигдé, никудá, никогдá,** and **никáк** do not decline.

2. **никакóй** declines in any gender, case, and number like an adjective with a velar stem (к). (**See** the chapter "Adjectives: Sample Declensions," section III, in this grammar for a detailed chart.)

3. **никтó** and **ничтó** decline just like **кто** and **что**. (**See** the chapter "Pronouns and Special Modifiers," section I, in this grammar for a detailed chart.)

4. When **кто, что,** and **никакóй** are **the object of a preposition**, the preposition goes between the prefix **ни** and the proper form of кто, что, or никакóй. This type of phrase is written as three separate words.

    a. Я **ни о ком** не говорю́. I'm not talking **about anyone**.
    b. Я **ни над чем** не рабóтаю I'm not working **on anything**.
    c. **Ни на какие** вопрóсы не отвечáй! Don't answer **any questions**.

II. Употреблéние—Use (p. 212)

A. Replying Negatively

1. "ни-" words give negative answers to questions posed by such question words as кто, что, какóй, где, кудá, когдá, and как.

2. **Remember: Do not give a negative answer** using forms with the particles -то and –нибудь. Always use negative (ни-) constructions.

3. Neutral word order for "ни-" words is before the verb.

    a. Мы **ни на когó** не жáлуемся. We aren't complaining **about anyone**.
    b. Они́ **никáк** не мóгут нам помóчь. They can't help us **at all**.

4. The verb in a sentence with a "ни-" word is always preceded by the negative particle **не**.

   a. Я **никуда не** иду. I'm **not** going **anywhere**.
   b. Они **никогда не** приходят к нам в гости. They **never** visit us.

B. More than One Negative

1. As you can see from previous examples, Russian employs double negatives. (Я **никуда не** иду.) Unlike in English, this is grammatically correct.

2. In Russian you may employ as many "ни–" words in one sentence as you like:
Я **никогда никуда не** хожу. = I **never** go **anywhere**.

C. In spoken Russian, the nominative form **ничто** is replaced by the genitive form **ничего**.

1. Здесь мне **ничего** не нравится. I don't like **anything** here.

2. Вам **ничего** не поможет.
Nothing will help you./**Nothing** is going to help you.

Real and Unreal Conditions

As in English, Russian can create conditional statements of the type "**If** A occurs, **then** so will B." Also just as in English, there are two types of conditional constructions in Russian: the **real** and the **unreal** (or statement contrary to fact). **Both are introduced by the conjunction éсли.**

I. The Real Conditional (pp. 157, 158)

A. Qualities

    1. It is a statement of fact referring to something that could (or did) take place.

    2. Verbs in the real conditional can be in past, present, or future tense. **Unlike in English,** however, the verbs in both clauses must be in the **same** tense. **For statements in the future, Russian uses future tense in both clauses**, whereas English uses present tense in the "if" clause. (**See** example I, B, 2, below.)

B. Examples

    1. Éсли тебé скýчно (present tense), иди́ домо́й. If you are bored, go home.

    2. Éсли у меня́ бýдут (**future** tense) дéньги, я куплю́ (future tense) маши́ну. If I have (**present** tense) the money, I will buy (future tense) the car.

    3. Éсли вы́ бы́ли больны́ (past tense), почемý вы ничего́ не сказа́ли (past)? If you were ill (past tense), why didn't (past tense) you say anything?

II. The Unreal Conditional (pp. 157, 158)

A. Qualities

    1. It is a statement about something that might take place but probably won't or that might have taken place but didn't.

    2. **Verbs** in both parts of the sentence **are in the past tense**, and both parts of the sentence use the conditional particle **бы** (which can be shortened to **б** in rapid speech).

B. Examples[1]

    1. Éсли бы они́ позвони́ли, я бы вам сказа́л.
    If they were to call (**but they probably won't**), I would tell you.
  OR If they had called (**but they didn't**), I would have told you.

    2. Éсли бы он пришёл во́время, мы пошли́ бы в кино́.
    If he comes on time (**but he probably won't**), we would go to the movies.
  OR If he had come on time (**but he didn't**), we would have gone to the movies.

---

[1] На ва́шем/твоём месте я бы . . . . = If I were you, I would . . . .

Sentence Structure

I. The Subject and the Predicate

Just as in English, a typical Russian sentence contains a **subject (подлежа́щее)** and a **predicate (сказу́емое)**.

A. Подлежа́щее—The Subject

1. In Russian, **subjects** are generally expressed in nominative case and answer the questions **Кто?** or **Что?** (p. 61)

    a. **Кто** рабо́тает в магази́не? В магази́не рабо́тает **моя́ дочь** (#).
    Who works in the store? **My daughter** works in the store.

    b. **Что** лежи́т на столе́? На столе́ лежи́т **ру́сский журна́л** (#).
    What is on the table? **A Russian magazine** is on the table.

2. Since **word order** in Russian is not fixed, the subject of a sentence does not always come at the beginning of the sentence. Generally, what is already known (that is, "old" information) comes first in a Russian sentence, and the unknown (or "new") information comes after it. In sentences a and b above, the subject is at the end of the sentence because in both instances it represents new information. In sentence a, for example, we already know from the question that someone is working in a store. In the answer, this is old information and therefore comes first (В магази́не рабо́тает . . .). The new information, which directly answers the question "Who?" (Кто?), comes at the end of the sentence (. . . моя́ дочь). (p. 63)

B. Сказу́емое—The Predicate (pp. 106–107)

1. **Definition:** In Russian the predicate denotes an action performed by the subject or anything that is said about the subject. It answers the questions **What does the subject do? What does the subject undergo? What (or who) is the subject?**

              subject   predicate
    a. Го́сти **пришли́**. The guests **have arrived**.
        Who? What did they do?

              subject   predicate
    b. Алекса́ндр — **инжене́р**. Alexander is **an engineer**.
        Who?   Who/What?

2. **Types of Predicates**

    a. **Verbal Predicates**

        1'. **Simple verbal predicates** are expressed with a verb.

            a'. Бо́ря **спал**. Boria **was sleeping**.
            b'. Ка́тя **чита́ет**. Katia **is reading**.

2'. Compound verbal predicates are expressed by an infinitive together with personal forms of the verb which indicate either the beginning or the end of the action or an intention, possibility, probability, wish, etc.

> a'. Он **на́чал чита́ть.** He **began reading (to read).**
> b'. Она́ **лю́бит пла́вать.** She **loves to swim.**

b. **Nominal predicates** are expressed by nouns or pronouns.

1'. Simple nominal predicates are expressed without a <u>linking verb</u> (auxiliary verb). (**Remember** that the present tense of быть is not expressed in Russian.)

> a'. Они́ **студе́нты.** They <u>**are**</u> **students.**
> b'. Он **космона́вт.** He <u>**is**</u> **a cosmonaut.**

2'. Compound nominal predicates are expressed with a <u>linking verb</u> (auxiliary verb). (**Remember:** Instrumental case is used after the past and present tenses and the infinitive of быть.)

> a'. Моя́ сестра́ **была́ фи́зиком.**
> My sister <u>**was**</u> **a physicist.**

> b'. Жена́ **рабо́тает врачо́м.**
> My wife <u>**works as**</u> **a doctor.**

> c'. Он **ста́нет учи́телем ру́сского языка́.**
> He <u>**is becoming**</u> (<u>**will be**</u>) **a Russian teacher.**

c. **Predicate Adjectives**

1'. Simple adjectival predicates, using either **long-** or **short-form** adjectives, are expressed without a <u>linking verb</u> (auxiliary verb).[1] (**Remember** that the present tense of быть is not expressed in Russian.)

> a'. Они́ **прия́тные.** They <u>**are**</u> **pleasant.**
> b'. Все студе́нты **больны́.** All the students <u>**are**</u> **sick.**

2'. Compound adjectival predicates, using either **long-** or **short-form** adjectives, are expressed with a <u>linking verb</u> (auxiliary verb). (**Remember:** Instrumental case is used after the past and present tenses and the infinitive of быть.)

> a'. Моя́ мла́дшая сестра́ <u>**бу́дет высо́кой.**</u>
> My younger sister <u>**will be**</u> **tall.**

> b'. Вчера́ ве́чером Ви́ктор Петро́вич **был сча́стлив.**
> Yesterday evening Viktor Petrovich <u>**was**</u> **happy.**

---

[1] For a review of both long- and short-form adjectives, **see** the chapter "Adjectives," section I, in this grammar.

II. Простые предложения—Simple Sentences

A simple sentence may either have only a subject or a predicate (a one-unit sentence) or both a subject and a predicate (a two-unit sentence).

A. One-Unit Sentences (p. 131)

1. Subject Only

a. **Ве́чер.** It's **evening**.

b. "**Ночь, у́лица, фона́рь, апте́ка . . .**"
"**Night, a street, a streetlight, a pharmacy . . .**"   Alexander Blok (1912)

2. Predicate Only

a. The **subject is omitted** because it is clear from the form of the verb and the context.

1'. **Чита́ю.** I'm **reading**.
2'. **Убира́ю** кварти́ру. I **am cleaning** my apartment.

b. A **third-person plural subject is omitted** to indicate the generalized subject of a verb. In such sentences the focus is on the action itself and not on the performer of the action. These sentences can be translated in either active or passive voice.

1'. Библиоте́ку **постро́или** в 1985-м году́.
They **built** the library in 1985. (active voice)
The library **was built** in 1985. (passive voice)

2'. Наш дом неда́вно **покра́сили**.
They recently **painted** our house. (active voice)
Our house **was** recently **painted**. (passive voice)

c. **Impersonal Sentences**

1'. **Impersonal Verbs**

a'. **Холода́ет.** It's **getting cold**.
b'. **Темне́ло.** It **was getting dark**.

2'. **ну́жно, на́до, нельзя́, мо́жно**, etc.[2]

(The logical subject goes in the dative case; бы́ло is used for the past tense, бу́дет for the future.)

a'. Здесь **нельзя́** кури́ть.
Smoking **is not permitted** here.

---

[2] For a fuller list of the forms from which impersonal statements can be created, **see** the chapter "Dative Case," section II, G, in this grammar.

dative
b'. Нам **на́до бы́ло** гото́виться к экза́мену.
We **had** to study for the exam.

B. Two-Unit Sentences: Subject and <u>Predicate</u> (p. 130)

subject predicate   subject predicate
1. **Они́** <u>пошли́</u> в кино́. **They** <u>went</u> to the movies.

subject   predicate
2. **Дом** <u>постро́ен</u> в восемна́дцатом ве́ке.

subject   predicate
The house <u>was built</u> in the eighteenth century.

III. Сло́жные предложе́ния—Complex Sentences

A. **то, что** (pp. 181–82)

This phrase links two clauses that both need to be completed grammatically. In each of the **English** sentences below, one pronoun can fill two different grammatical roles. For example, in sentence 3, "what" is both the object of the preposition "about" and the direct object of the verb "promised." This situation is permissible in English but not in Russian. Because **Russian** has case endings, one word cannot go into two different cases (in sentence 3 this would be prepositional and accusative). The solution to this problem is the combination **то, что.** As **pronouns** in this construction, **то** and **что** both decline to fulfill the grammatical requirements of their respective clauses. Thus, in sentence 3, **то** goes into prepositional case as the object of the preposition **о**, and **что** goes into accusative case as the direct object of обеща́ть. **то, что** is most often translated as "what" or "that which." **Note** that the pronoun **что** is stressed and the **о** is pronounced **o** when **что** is the subject or direct object.

1. Мы купи́ли **то, что́** бы́ло ну́жно.   **то** (acc.) direct object of купи́ть
We bought **what (that which)** we needed.   **что** (nom.) subject of clause

2. **То, что́** они́ говоря́т, мне не нра́вится.   **то** (nom.) subject of verb нра́виться
I don't like **what** they are saying.   **что** (acc.) direct object of говори́ть

3. Вы забы́ли о **том, что́** вы обеща́ли.   **том** (prep.) object of preposition **о**
You forgot about **what** you promised.   **что** (acc.) direct object of обеща́ть

4. Я интересу́юсь **тем, что́** они́ де́лают.   **тем** (instr.) obj. of интересова́ться
I'm interested in **what** they are doing.   **что** (acc.) direct object of де́лать

B. "Before" and "After": **до, пе́ред,** and **по́сле** vs. **до того́ как, пе́ред тем как,** and **по́сле того́ как** (p. 183)

The **English** words "before" and "after" are both prepositions and conjunctions. **In Russian,** you must distinguish between the **prepositions до, пе́ред,** and **по́сле** and the **conjunctions до того́ как, пе́ред тем как,** and **по́сле того́ как.** Prepositions are followed by pronouns or (adjectives and) nouns; conjunctions introduce a new clause or, in the case of **пе́ред тем как,** can also be followed by an infinitive.

1. **Preposition vs. Conjunction**

Preposition	Conjunction	Meaning
до + genitive case	до того́ как + clause	(anytime) **before**
пе́ред + instrumental case	пе́ред тем как + clause or infinitive	(just) **before**
по́сле + genitive case	по́сле того́ как + clause	**after**

2. **Examples**

   a. **Prepositions**

              genitive
      1'. **До** войны́ Ни́на Влади́мировна жила́ в Ленингра́де.
      Before the war Nina Vladimirovna lived in Leningrad.

             instrumental
      2'. **Пе́ред** уро́ком они́ говори́ли друг с дру́гом.
      They talked with each other (**right**) **before class**.

             genitive
      3'. **По́сле** конца́ семе́стра на́ша семья́ пое́дет на Кавка́з.
      Our family is going to the Caucasus **after the end** of the semester.

   b. **Conjunctions**

             new clause
      1'. **До того́ как** Ми́ша перее́хал в Москву́, он рабо́тал здесь.
      Before Misha moved to Moscow, he worked here.

                         new clause
      2'. Моя́ тётя начала́ рабо́тать в ба́нке **по́сле того́, как** она́ око́нчила университе́т.

      My aunt began working at the bank **after** she graduated from college.

                    new clause
      3'. Ната́ша звони́ла мне **пе́ред тем, как** она́ се́ла обе́дать.
      Natasha called me **before** she began eating dinner.

             OR

             infinitive
      4'. **Пе́ред тем как** сесть обе́дать, Ната́ша звони́ла мне.
      Before sitting down to dinner, Natasha called me.

C. **"It depends on . . . .": зави́сеть от + genitive case** (p. 182)

1. When a **conjunction** is needed to join this expression to another **clause**, use **зави́сеть от того́ + что** or **как** or **. . . ли.**

             genitive acc.
  a. Э́то зави́сит **от того́, что́** они ска́жут. **что** (acc.) dir. obj. of сказа́ть
  It depends **on what** they say.

genitive   new clause
b. Мой отвéт завúсит **от тогó**, придýт **ли** онú.
My answer depends **on whether** (**or not**) they come.

genitive   new clause
c. Всё завúсит **от тогó**, **как** он готóвится к экзáмену.
Everything depends **on how** he prepares for the final.

2. When only a **noun** or **pronoun** is needed to complete the sentence, add it in **genitive case** after the preposition **от** (завúсеть от **когó/чегó**).

genitive
a. Всё завúсит **от** погóд**ы**.
Everything depends **on the weather**.

gen.
b. Э́то завúсит **от вас**. This depends **on you**.

D. "Instead of" Doing Something: вмéсто тогó чтóбы + infinitive (p. 184)

1. **Вмéсто тогó чтóбы смотрéть** фильм, мы идём на лéкцию.
Instead of seeing a film, we are going to a lecture.

2. **Вмéсто тогó чтóбы пойтú** на урóк, я спал.
Instead of going to my lesson, I slept.

E. The Conjunction что (p. 182)

An unstressed **что** (the vowel is pronounced as a schwa [shtə]) is a **conjunction** that is the equivalent of the English "that." In English we often omit this conjunction, but it cannot be omitted in Russian. As a conjunction, **что** introduces a new clause. It is not the subject of the clause, nor is it the object of a verb or preposition in its clause. For these reasons, it does not decline when used this way. Sometimes this unchanging form is preceded by a clause that utilizes the pronoun "**то**." (**See** examples in E, 2, below.)

1. When the Preceding Clause Does Not Require "то"

new clause
a. Онá сказáла, **что** Пýшкин её любúмый поэ́т.
She said (**that**) Pushkin is her favorite poet.

new clause
b. Детú знáют, **что** гóсти приезжáют сегодня вéчером.
The children know (**that**) our guests are arriving tonight.

2. When the Preceding Clause Requires the Use of "то"

Clauses introduced by the unstressed **conjunction что** or other conjunctive words (**как, когдá, ли**) are often preceded by the **pronoun** "**то**" in order to complete the grammatical requirements of the preceding clause. The case of "**то**" is determined by the preposition or verb that governs it.

new clause

a. Дéло в **том, что** мы егó не знáем. **том** (prep.) object of **в**
The fact of the matter is (**that**) we don't know him.

new clause

b. Мы соглáсны с **тем, что** он прекрáсный студéнт. **тем** (instrumental)
We agree **that** he is an excellent student. object of **с**

F. The Conjunction **как** in the Phrases "**I saw. . .**" and "**I heard. . .**" (p. 145)

Use the **conjunction как** to begin a new clause with a subject and verb that describes what the subject in the initial clause saw or heard.

new clause

1. Я вúдела, **как онú танцевáли**. I saw **them dancing**.

new clause

2. Я слы́шал, **как Нúна говорúт** с Мáрком.
I heard **Nina talking** with Mark.

G. The Conjunction **ли** (p. 88)

ли is a **conjunction** equivalent to the English conjunctions "**whether**" and "**if**."[3]

1. Use

   a. **ли** always comes **after** the word(s) it calls into question.

   b. The word called into question by **ли** comes at the beginning of its clause.

2. Examples

new clause

a. Мы ещё не знáем, придёт **ли** он.
We still don't know **whether** (**or not**) he's coming.

new clause

b. Кто знáет, звонúла **ли** Лéна сегóдня?
Who knows **if** Lena called today?

---

[3] In addition, **ли** is an interrogative particle that is used to make questions more polite and slightly more formal:
Знáете ли вы, где нахóдится библиотéка? (Do you know [Would you happen to know] where the library is?)
(p. 103)

Словообразова́ние—Word Formation

I. Nouns

A. **Diminutive** Suffixes (p. 127)

1. Masculine: -**ик**, -**чик**, -**ок**

   a. сто́л**ик** = a **little** table
   b. стака́н**чик** = a **small** glass
   c. городо́**к** = a **small** city

2. Feminine: -**к**(а), -**ичк**(а)

   a. ко́мнат**ка** = a **small** room
   b. води́**чка** = water (adds emotional connotation of humor or affection)

B. The suffixes -**ец** (masculine) and -**к**(а) (feminine) denote **nationality** (p. 192).

1. Укра́йна → украи́**нец**, украи́**нка** (a Ukrainian)
2. Аме́рика → америка́**нец**, америка́**нка** (an American)
3. А́фрика → африка́**нец**, африка́**нка** (an African)

But:
4. Болга́рия → болга́рин, болга́рка (a Bulgarian)
5. Ла́твия → латы́ш, латы́шка (a Latvian)
6. По́льша → поля́к, по́лька (a Pole)
7. Че́хия → чех, че́шка (a Czech)
8. Се́рбия → серб, се́рбка (a Serbian)
9. Хорва́тия → хорва́т, хорва́тка (a Croatian)
10. Слова́кия → слова́к, слова́чка (a Slovak)

C. The suffixes -**ист** (masculine) and -**истк**(а) (feminine) denote people **who play instruments** or **sports.**

1. **Players of Instruments**

   a. саксофо́н → саксофон**и́ст**, саксофон**и́стка** (saxophone player)
   b. гита́ра → гитар**и́ст**, гитар**и́стка** (guitarist)
   c. пиани́но → пиан**и́ст**, пиан**и́стка** (piano player)
   d. а́рфа → арф**и́ст**, арф**и́стка** (harpist)

2. **Players of Sports** (p. 316)

   a. те́ннис → теннис**и́ст**, теннис**и́стка** (tennis player)
   b. баскетбо́л → баскетбол**и́ст**, баскетбол**и́стка** (basketball player)
   c. ша́хматы → шахмат**и́ст**, шахмат**и́стка** (chess player)
   d. хокке́й → хокке**и́ст**, хокке**и́стка** (hockey player)

D. Suffixes that Make **Verbs into Nouns**

   1. The suffixes -**тель** (masculine) and -**ниц**(а) (feminine) designate **the doer of an action** (p. 198).

a. писа́ть	→	писа́**тель**, писа́**тельниц**а (writer)
b. учи́ть	→	учи́**тель**, учи́**тельниц**а (teacher)
c. чита́ть	→	чита́**тель**, чита́**тельниц**а (reader)
d. жи́ть	→	жи́**тель**, жи́**тельниц**а (inhabitant)

   2. The Suffix -**а́ни**(е) (p. 46)

a. око́нчить	→	оконча́**ни**е (graduation)
b. зада́ть	→	зада́**ни**е (assignment)
c. преподава́ть	→	преподава́**ни**е (teaching)
d. собра́ть	→	собра́**ни**е (gathering, meeting)

   3. The Suffix -**е́ни**(е) (p. 87)

a. пригласи́ть	→	приглаше́**ни**е (invitation)
b. сочини́ть	→	сочине́**ни**е (composition)
c. объяви́ть	→	объявле́**ни**е (announcement)
d. произноси́ть	→	произноше́**ни**е (pronunciation)

E. Suffixes that Make **Adjectives into Nouns**

   1. The Suffixes -**ик** (masculine) and -**иц**(а) (feminine)

a. совреме́нный	→	совреме́н**ник**, совреме́н**ниц**а (contemporary)
b. отли́чный	→	отли́ч**ник**, отли́ч**ниц**а (excellent student)

   2. The suffix -**ость** makes adjectives into **feminine дверь-type abstract nouns** (p. 14).

a. тру́дный	→	тру́дн**ость** (difficulty)
b. но́вый	→	но́в**ость** (news, novelty)
c. молодо́й	→	мо́лод**ость** (youth)
d. специа́льный	→	специа́льн**ость** (specialty)

II. Adjectives

A. Suffixes that Make **Adjectives out of Nouns**

   1. The Suffix -**н**- (pp. 2, 103, 112, 314)

a. те́ннис	→	те́ннис**н**ая раке́тка (tennis racket)
b. баскетбо́л	→	баскетбо́ль**н**ый корт (basketball court)
c. хокке́й	→	хокке́й**н**ые коньки́ (hockey skates)
d. за́пад	→	за́пад**н**ый штат (a Western state)

2. The Suffix -и́ческ- (p. 2)

a. биоло́гия	→	биологи́ческий (biological)
b. исто́рия	→	истори́ческий (historic[al])
c. филосо́фия	→	философи́ческий (philosophical)
d. эконо́мия	→	экономи́ческий (economic)

Note: Since Russian is an inflected language, you may not use one noun to qualify a second noun that **follows** it. In English, it is permissible to say "bus stop" and "tennis racket." In these phrases the **nouns** "bus" and "tennis" qualify the nouns that follow them. In Russian, this is not acceptable. To use one noun to qualify another you have two options: 1) turn the first noun into an adjective, such as in II, A, 1–2, above, or 2) place the qualifying noun **in genitive case after** the noun it qualifies, such as in the phrase остано́вка авто́буса (**bus** stop).

B. **Compound adjectives** can be formed in the following ways:

1. To link two adjectives, add an -**o** ending to the stem of the first adjective and join it to the second adjective by means of a hyphen (pp. 102, 127).

a. ру́сско-англи́йский слова́рь = a Russian-English dictionary
b. чёрно-бе́лый телеви́зор = a black-and-white television
c. тёмно-си́ний костю́м = a dark blue (navy blue) suit
d. си́не-зелёная вода́ = blue-green water

2. To use the numeral "one" to form a compound adjective, add the neuter nominative form of the numeral (одно́) to the adjective (p. 112).

a. одномото́рный самолёт = a **single**-engine aircraft
b. одноа́ктная пье́са = a **one**-act play

3. To use a cardinal numeral other than "one" (two, three, four, five, etc.) to form a compound adjective, add the **genitive** form of the number (двух, трёх, четырёх, пяти́) to the adjective (p. 112).[1]

a. двухэта́жный дом = a **two**-story house
b. трёхко́мнатная кварти́ра = a **three**-room apartment
c. пятиле́тний план = a **five**-year plan

C. The Suffix -еньк- /-оньк- imparts a **diminutive** meaning to an adjective (or adverb) and usually an affectionate **emotional coloring** as well. In some contexts, this suffix can express a negative or unfavorable attitude. (p. 153)

1. ми́лый (sweet, nice)	→	ми́ленький (sweet, nice, darling)
2. молодо́й (young)	→	моло́денький (young, very young)
3. ти́хо (quietly, softly)	→	тихо́нько (quietly, softly)

---

[1] For a review of the genitive case of cardinal numerals, see the chapter "Review: The Declension of Numerals," sections I–VI, in this grammar.

III. Verbs

A. The prefix **пере-** imparts the meaning of doing something **again** (p. 321).

1. **пере**сказа́ть = to **re**tell
2. **пере**звони́ть = to phone **again**
3. **пере**спроси́ть = to ask **again**

B. The prefix **по-** imparts the meaning of doing something **for a short time** (p. 322).

1. **по**говори́ть = to talk **for a while**
2. **по**ходи́ть = to walk **for a while**
3. **по**сиде́ть = to sit **for a short time**